THE QUANTUM LEAP

Activate Your Genius by Reprogramming Your Subconscious

Mark Scherer, PhD

Published by Project ICON

Cover design by: Lars Doerwarld

Digital ISBN: 978-1-969888-19-9
Paperback ISBN: 978-1-969888-21-2
Hardback ISBN: 978-1-969888-20-5

https://projecticon.io/

Table of Contents

Foreword

What if the single greatest obstacle to your ease, peace, happiness, or success is not a lack of effort, a painful past, or a flaw in your design, but something in your subconscious, something based on an illusion, and something that you can change more easily than you might ever imagine?

For centuries, humanity has lived within the story of separation: the belief that we "fell from grace" and were exiled from Adam and Eve's paradise into a world of opposites: right and wrong, good and evil, punishment and reward. Dr. Mark Scherer invites us to see this not as history, but as metaphor. The "fall" was never a punishment; it was the moment we began believing we were separate from Source, separate from love, and separate from one another. It was the moment we bit into the apple of judgment.

Most people live unaware that the walls confining them are made of their own words, thoughts, and feelings. In *The Quantum Leap*, Dr. Scherer reveals how our subconscious addiction to emotional pain, fueled by the language of judgment ("this is right," "that is wrong," "this shouldn't have happened", "you're not enough"), creates powerful biochemical cycles of shame, blame, guilt, and hate or resentment. These emotions bind us to old narratives and stuck patterns, reinforcing the illusion of the limitations we subconsciously place upon ourselves, and that hold us back from the life we yearn for. The power lies in the fact that these patterns and emotions also contain the keys to our understanding awakening. Dr. Scherer reveals that our stuck patterns and the symptoms they produce are truly blessings, revealing underlying emotions and patterns requiring attention, that can reveal the transformational beauty waiting for each of us willing to do the work.

Through decades of experience, research and practice, Dr. Scherer has developed the Quantum Leap Technique (QLT), a synthesis of neuroscience, quantum physics, experiential psychology, and spiritual wisdom. His work is innovative and truly life-changing, awakening the dormant genius within each person, and provides a clear, evidence-informed pathway to dissolve emotional barriers and reprogram subconscious patterns that govern perception, emotion and performance. The result is a profound shift from unconscious reactivity to conscious co-creation. We have the power within us to co-create the beautiful life that is available to each of us.

The essential question becomes: Are we creating from unconscious conditioning or from conscious choice? Dr. Scherer demonstrates that the key to transformation is not effort, strategy, positivity, or even forgiveness; it is based on conscious assessments, seeing and acting on our own role in loving ourselves and changing our 3-D reality, being grateful, seeing daily miracles all around us, and most of all by understanding our own subconscious programming, and transforming it to conscious programming. This allows us to transform our lives, revealing enthusiasm, ease, joy, and success beyond anything we could previously imagine. Truly seeing through a Quantum Leap consciousness lens allows us to perceive the inherent intelligence within every experience, instantly changing our outcomes by changing our reactions, dissolving the emotional charge of the past, and revealing life as a purposeful, responsive mirror. When perception changes, the story changes, and our lives are transformed.

This transformation has been experienced by countless individuals participating in Dr. Scherer and Encompass Life's classes, coaching, and in-person intensive experiences. Lives are transformed through this approach. Ongoing qEEG analysis and other research are helping us understand from a neuroscience perspective what exactly is going on in the brain, behind that transformation. These are exciting times!

Quantum Leap coaching offers a model for transformation that is as scientific as it is spiritual, and as practical as it is profound. It challenges traditional self-improvement paradigms and provides a coherent framework for individuals, coaches, leaders, and seekers ready to facilitate or achieve genuine, lasting change, not through more doing, but through deeper alignment with the subconscious intelligence and spiritual promises of life itself.

Being involved in this work myself feels like standing on the threshold of possibility, where science and soul converge, and the path to ease and joy is not upward or outward, but inward. As a medical practitioner who works with complex chronic mental, developmental, neurologic, and physical illness, and who has seen lives transformed by this method, I wholeheartedly recommend this approach, as well as Mark and his team. I have seen major improvements in my own life through studying consciousness and my involvement in the Encompass Life courses and intensive immersive experiences. I'm also thrilled that my learning is leading to improved outcomes for my toughest patients. Mark and his team are caring, skilled, and confident in uncovering their clients' root emotional and spiritual underpinnings and stuck, subconscious patterns, and as a result, transforming their relationships, performance, careers, and finances. I strongly recommend Mark and his team as master quantum leap coaches and teachers. If you are ready to transcend struggle, improve your health, save your marriage, or reach the pinnacle of success, you are in the right place. Your quantum leap begins now.

Chapter 1: Beyond Right and Wrong

The Fall from Grace: Adam, Eve, and the Original Illusion

What if I told you that the root of all the pain, confusion, and suffering we experience, personally and collectively, can be traced back to one single moment? One choice. One illusion. That ancient story, the one we've heard in churches and children's books, about Adam and Eve and the Tree of the Knowledge of Good and Evil, holds far more wisdom than we were ever taught to believe. It's not just a tale about temptation or punishment; it's a metaphor for the very birth of duality, the moment we collectively believed we fell out of unity and into the illusion of separation.

Most people grow up hearing a version of the story that paints God as a vengeful being who banished Adam and Eve from paradise because they disobeyed. From that moment on, we're told, humanity has suffered under the weight of that original sin, a fall from grace that cursed the rest of us to a life of toil, pain, and punishment; however, that never sat right with me.

I remember, as a kid, right around the time I found out Santa Claus was fake, I was sitting in the back seat of my parents' car while they talked about God. I had similarly been told Santa might leave you a lump of coal for misbehaving. It felt absurd. My young brain couldn't reconcile the idea of a loving, all-knowing Creator with the image of an angry cosmic figure tallying my sins and ready to sentence me to eternal fire for getting it wrong. My heart pondered and longed for a greater Truth yet to be revealed.

This began a 30-year study of transforming who God was NOT to who God IS in his core being and nature. Part of this included me questioning the narrative of what I was taught. Some of the next questions I asked are as follows:

What if Adam and Eve were never actually kicked out of Eden? What if paradise wasn't taken from them, but they simply stopped believing they belonged there?

That was the shift that changed everything for me: the idea that it wasn't punishment, but perception, that caused their exile. They didn't lose Eden; they lost their awareness of it. It was not their behavior, but their belief in separation that cast them out of Eden.

When they ate from the Tree of the Knowledge of Good and Evil, they stepped into the language of "This is right, that is wrong, I am good, you are bad," and also stepped out of unity into judgment. That was the real fall. This was also the birth of duality at the moment they started believing things were happening to them rather than through them or for them. And once that seed of separation took root in human consciousness, it grew and grew. Layer upon layer of falsehood was built upon that single lie.

Scripture says that God is truth. God is light. God is life. God is love. If that's the case, then lies, darkness, and death are simply the absence of God's presence. I often ask people in my classes, "Have you ever been anywhere that life wasn't?" They pause. Some think of the desert. Others imagine outer space. But eventually I ask, "Are you alive?" And they nod. "Then life is here." You can't be somewhere life isn't, because life isn't something you step into. It's something you are. Your heart is beating right now, and you don't have to tell it to beat. It does it all on its own without words. It beats, and then it beats faster when someone you love walks by. You don't think that into being; it just is. That's life and God's design.

Every state of mental fog, stress, disease, and scarcity I've ever seen stems from the same root: the belief in separation and the language that belief generates.

Adam and Eve's story is not ancient history; it's a mirror. The same two choices are offered to each of us every single day. Will we eat from the tree of judgment, the illusion of duality? Or will we stay rooted in the truth of oneness, the knowing that we are co-creators with the divine?

You've likely heard of the law of attraction. But here, we teach something even more profound: We teach that you were created in the image of God. This means that you are a creator too! Call it God, Source, or Spirit. The energy from which all things are created is the very energy you're made from. And because of that, you have the power to create with it. Interestingly enough, you are always creating! Sometimes you create from lack, fear, or rage. These tend to be unconscious creations from feelings of hate, shame, and frustration. Once you begin to wake up to your divine co-creator gifts, you can consciously learn (or remember!) to create from joy, peace, and love itself, activating the genius that has always lived within you!

Because whatever emotion you create from becomes infused in what you create. If you build a life out of anger, you will live in a world that makes you angry. If you build it from resentment, then resentment will line the walls of every room you walk into in the process, not as a punishment, but as a mirror. God designed this perfect feedback system not to shame nor punish you; he created it to wake you up. In this way, you can clearly see what you're using your divine power to create.

This creates a change in perspective from victimhood to ownership, where your power begins. For example, the question, "Why do I keep attracting these kinds of people or experiences?" is replaced with a practical and truthful question: "What part of me is drawn to this?" When I hear the answer, I have power over the emotional blockage and can make changes.

Even the way we speak about these forces matters. Try saying, "the law of attraction." Now say, "the gift of attraction." Feel the difference? One feels rigid, like a rule. The other feels generous and inviting, like a sacred technology. That's not semantics. That's energy. That's frequency. That's how creation responds to God's voice of truth in you.

Every word we speak is either an act of separation or an act of unity. Every sentence either denies life or breathes life. Lies, especially the ones we quietly agree to drain us. They fracture our energy, they disempower us. Truth restores. It aligns us. It connects us back to the infinite stream we always have been in.

Look at the world around you. In any system where costs are going up while effectiveness is going down, you can almost always trace it back to a disconnection from truth. For example, look at healthcare or education. We keep pouring money into solutions that don't heal and don't teach. Why? Because the systems are built on faulty beliefs. Beliefs rooted in separation are characterized by a cycle of fear, shame, and control.

Einstein said it well: You cannot solve problems with the same thinking that created them. And yet we keep trying to fix issues externally. What we're doing here is different; we're not applying new thoughts to an old paradigm. We're waking up from the paradigm altogether.

To me, it's like a computer that once had a brilliant operating system, one of pure unity, love, and truth, but over time it became infected. The virus didn't destroy the system. It just layered over it, slowed it down, and corrupted its files. But the original system is still underneath the dysfunction. It is still intact and perfectly whole.

When you run a virus scan, you start to see all the corrupted files. These essentially are all the lies you've inherited and the beliefs that don't belong to you. And as you clear them by bringing them to the light, they dissolve. Then something beautiful happens: The original programming, the one you were born with, begins to function again.

Yes, the one wired for harmony, creation and joy begins to truly thrive.

This is what we're doing. We're scanning for the virus. The patterns. The hidden beliefs that distort our truth and steal our peace.

That virus shows up in feelings like jealousy, rage, blame, resentment. These emotions aren't evil; they're signs. They tell you that something inside is making life wrong. Something inside you is living in judgment instead of truth. And judgment always leads to complaint. Complaint builds up until the body breaks, toxicity spills over into illness, and until separation turns into suffering.

But the invitation is always the same: Return. Remember. Reclaim the Eden you never actually left and always have been living!

Because the real fall wasn't disobedience. It was forgetfulness. And the real redemption begins the moment you remember who you are.

The Hidden Trap of Duality: Why "Good vs. Bad" Keeps Us Stuck

When a person begins living inside the illusion of good versus bad, right versus wrong, something subtle but devastating begins to occur. It's not always immediate. At first, it can even feel righteous. Just like Adam and Eve in the Garden, it starts with a bite of awareness, a taste of judgment. But what follows is far more than a moral framework; it is an emotional trap. And once we step into that illusion, a hidden operating system begins to run in the background of our lives. That system is fueled not by clarity, but by distortion. And it doesn't bring us closer to love, truth, or healing. It locks us in place.

At the core of this illusion lives a sticky, unseen web woven from four deeply charged emotions: shame, blame, guilt, and hate. These aren't just feelings; they're biochemical traps. They are the emotional glue that holds our most limiting patterns in place. And once they take root, even the most powerful intentions to change, on their own, won't be enough to break free.

Over the years, I've learned that whenever someone is stuck in a repeating pattern, a chronic behavior, belief, or self-sabotaging loop, those four emotions are always there, quietly operating behind the scenes. Rather than trying to force the pattern to shift by sheer will or logic, we must work to gently and skillfully dissolve the glue. When shame, blame, guilt, and hate begin to soften, the pattern starts to move on its own. That's when transformation happens, not by fixing, but by freeing.

Here's the metaphor I use: Imagine a jigsaw puzzle. If you take a finished puzzle and coat the back with superglue, that puzzle becomes one solid, immovable piece. Try to pry it apart, and you'll destroy it. But if the puzzle is old, worn, and loose, if the glue has worn off, it will fall apart with barely any effort. Patterns behave the same way. The tighter the grip of those four emotions, the stronger the glue. And the stronger the glue, the harder it is for the puzzle to come undone.

Shame is often the stickiest of them all. The more shame someone carries around a particular behavior or belief, the more likely they are to repeat it. It may not necessarily be in the same exact form, but in some variation that reactivates the same emotion. You might not do the exact thing again, but you'll likely find yourself doing something else that triggers the same internal ache. Why? Because the system is still glued together. Because you're still inside the lie.

And make no mistake, it is a lie. The illusion of right versus wrong is not truth; it's a distortion of reality. And that distortion gives rise to a self-sustaining chemical cycle within the body, a cycle that feels like morality on the surface but is actually addiction in disguise.

The body is a chemical factory. It can produce life-giving compounds that promote healing, connection, joy, and expansion. Or it can manufacture emotional toxins that mimic the effects of addictive drugs. The irony? These emotional chemicals are self-produced. And they're just as habit-forming, if not more, than any substance you could snort, swallow, drink, or inject.

You can become addicted to your emotional pain.

When someone chooses an external substance (cocaine, alcohol, or prescription meds), the act is visible. There's an identifiable moment: the sniff, the sip, the swallow. The outside world can see it, and so can the individual. But when the body becomes hooked on its own drama, its biochemical cocktail of shame or hate or guilt, the addiction flies under the radar. It looks like a personality trait. It sounds like a story you've been telling for years. It feels like you. That's what makes it so insidious.

You don't know you're hooked, because the drug lives inside your own emotional identity.

Most people, of course, don't like these emotions; they hate them. However, they've never been taught to view hate as an inherent part of the system itself. Any form of dislike, when taken to its root, is a form of hate. When someone is trapped in the right-versus-wrong paradigm, they're taught that hate is wrong. And what do we do with what's wrong? We suppress it.

Suppression, though, is not healing. It's hiding. And what we hide doesn't disappear, it festers. When we make something wrong, we lose the ability to admit it's even there. And when we can't realize it, we can't transform it. That unacknowledged hate, shame, or guilt begins to drive us, subtly shaping our choices, our language, our relationships. We begin to become the very emotion we've refused to acknowledge. The emotion owns us.

I remember growing up in a house where we weren't allowed to say the word *hate*. It was considered a bad word, something ugly and forbidden. But does that mean there was no hate in our home? No. In fact, it was everywhere: Even though the hate wasn't on the surface, it was hidden beneath. Because what is not allowed becomes what is most active in the unseen places. It leaks out in passive aggression, outbursts, manipulation, withdrawal, sarcasm, or judgment. And the body remembers it all.

When someone is filled with unprocessed hate, especially if they believe that hate is wrong, they will almost always find a way to numb it or project it. For some, that looks like drugs, alcohol, sex, or food. For others, it's overreaction, lashing out, or a slow erosion of their health. Whether it shows up as overt or covert hostility, the consequences are the same: sabotage. Sabotage in relationships. Sabotage in income. Sabotage in health. All of it stemming from an emotional prison they didn't know they were living in.

The tragedy is, this pattern becomes addictive. And just as a drug addict will lie to get another hit, so too will someone addicted to drama lie to themselves. They'll lie to others. They'll twist the truth to stay in the chemical state that has become familiar and safe. Even the lie gives them a fix. And when you're addicted to the lie, healing looks threatening.

You've probably seen people who appear highly functional, people who get results, build businesses, lead movements, or pursue success with relentless drive, but they're still operating from the same emotional addictions. Anger becomes a motivator. Hate fuels ambition. Shame becomes proof they must try harder to be enough. And because the world applauds performance and results, nobody notices the cost until the body breaks.

Eventually, the internal toxicity spills over. It starts with fatigue, maybe a chronic tension that won't go away. Then come the health issues, autoimmune disease, joint degeneration, digestive issues, early signs of Alzheimer's, and even structural breakdowns in the body. Why? Because emotion is not just psychological; it is physiological. And suppression doesn't delete chemistry. It multiplies it.

We weren't designed to live this way. We weren't meant to become trapped inside our own chemical responses, repeating patterns like prisoners of invisible shame. But the longer we live in the lie of judgment, the more natural it feels. And unless the glue is addressed, the pattern will hold. Until love returns to the system, truth won't move. Until we stop making our humanity wrong, healing can't begin. So, this isn't about fixing the pattern. It's about dissolving what holds it together. And when that happens, the truth doesn't need to be forced; it reveals itself.

The lie collapses. And with it, so does the addiction.

From Judgment to Unity: Redefining How We See Life

When we live through the lens of separation, seeing life in binaries, speaking in judgments, breathing in "right and wrong," we unknowingly poison our system. It's subtle at first, like a low hum in the background of a song, barely noticeable but always present. Before long, we find ourselves walking around in an invisible fog, a sea of complaints we don't even realize we're swimming in.

There's a study from Stanford that shines a harsh light on this phenomenon. It found that the simple act of complaining, whether actively doing it or passively listening to it for just thirty minutes, actually causes damage to our neurons. Real neurological damage. In other words, complaining literally makes us dumber. The brain begins to fire only along pre-established neural grooves. The pathways of thought become rigid, mechanical. Mainly, when triggered, the brain reacts in a snap, repeating a pattern it's rehearsed a thousand times before. No new awareness. No conscious choice and freedom. Just stimulus and reaction.

This reflexive loop, a stimulus-response chain, isn't random. It was formed early, often before we even had the words to explain what was happening. For some, the wiring begins as early as two or three years old. A traumatic moment occurs. A rupture of trust. A sudden abandonment. A confused silence. And the only way the child knows how to survive it is to wrap the experience in a cocoon of "not" statements: *It's not my fault. This shouldn't be happening. Life's not supposed to be like this.*

In the absence of a safe, integrated adult to co-regulate with, the child creates their own defense. They assign blame outside themselves in order to keep going. It's not immaturity; it's genius. That coping strategy allows the system to stay intact. But as the years go on, that strategy solidifies. What was once a survival mechanism becomes a reactive identity. Every time something similar happens, the nervous system reactivates. The reaction becomes a story. The story becomes a belief. The belief becomes a way of life.

What many don't realize is that this is more than an emotional reflex. It's a physiological state. The body gets locked into fight or flight. The sympathetic nervous system stays active. Although there is no real danger, the system stays braced, not because the danger is real, but because the story is still running. That story becomes the filter through which all of life is experienced. And from that filter, everything feels personal. Everything feels unsafe.

Many healing modalities speak of forgiveness. And yes, forgiveness can loosen the grip. It may reduce the charge, soften the sting, even open the door to a new chapter. Something beyond forgiveness is required to bring freedom. I've seen this time and again in my work with clients who have done years, decades, of forgiveness work, therapy, prayer, and processing. And still, they're stuck.

Some of the individuals I've worked with have endured the darkest traumas imaginable, experiences so painful they're almost unspeakable. MK-Ultra survivors. Individuals who lived through satanic ritual abuse. People whose emotional systems were shattered by experiences few could even fathom. And yet, many of them had already done "the work." They had forgiven their abusers. They had journaled, meditated, prayed. And still, the patterns persisted.

That's when I developed what I call the Quantum Leap Technique™ (QLT), a proven proprietary transformational method integrating unique tools for shifting thoughts, words, and feelings. This is a method that operates outside linear time and conventional therapeutic approaches. Unlike traditional healing modalities that work within the framework of processing trauma over months or years, QLT™ accesses transformation from what can only be described as a different dimensional plane.

Rooted in scriptural truths and aligned with insights from quantum physics, QLT bridges both spiritual and scientific understanding to accelerate transformation. The technique recognizes that as long as someone remains trapped in "this is wrong, that shouldn't have happened," they're biochemically bound to their trauma, literally addicted to the emotions of judgment. It allows individuals to revisit their experiences not as victims of circumstance, but as souls reclaiming their inherent power.

How It Works: In this rapid process, clients are empowered to separate from their stories, discover the purpose behind an incident, and reach a place of deep gratitude through an encounter with divine love. QLT works by facilitating access to a perspective outside of time and duality, where experiences can be seen through the lens of spiritual evolution rather than personal punishment. This allows them to instantly see the lesson and blessing in situations that once felt painful or traumatic. From this vantage point, the biochemical grip of shame, blame, guilt, and hate naturally dissolves because the story that feeds them has been fundamentally altered. Once the purpose is revealed, the next step is to envision a future built on this new meaning and begin taking aligned steps toward a transformed life.

That's when we began working with the QLT, and what happened next was beyond explanation.

In 20 to 30 minutes, something shifted. Not because we bypassed the pain, but because we accessed it from a different plane. For the first time, they could revisit the experience not as a victim of circumstance, but as a soul reclaiming power. And from that vantage point, outside of time, outside of the old story, they could do something radical.

They thanked the person. They thanked God. They found the blessing in the horror.

This is not spiritual bypassing. It's not dissociation or denial. It's the moment when the soul sees clearly: Nothing happens *to* me; it all happens *for* me. That recognition doesn't erase the pain. But it transforms the meaning, and meaning heals.

Results: As transformation unfolds, the body begins to restore itself, relationships flourish in both giving and receiving love, and areas such as money, creativity, and intuition naturally expand. By rewiring the brain and establishing new neurological pathways, QLT creates lasting shifts in behavior, health, relationships, and finances, restoring ease, peace, and the ability to consciously co-create reality through the remembrance of an intimate experience with love.

Gratitude, not forgiveness, is the key that finally unlocks the door. When someone finds the blessing inside the wound, the pattern no longer owns them. The person transforms because the blessing is the lesson. And once the lesson is received, the story no longer needs to be repeated.

It reminds me of the ancient saying: Everything in life is either a burden or a blessing. It all begins as a blessing; it only becomes a burden when we have yet to see the gift it carries. Forgiveness can lessen the weight, but only gratitude lifts it.

We are spiritual beings having a human experience. That's not just a nice quote for a coffee mug; it's the framework for understanding all healing. If we're stuck in the 3D realm of judgment, constantly assessing who's right, who's wrong, what's good, what's bad, we are living inside a prison of our own making. And the bars of that prison? They're made of words. Stories. Perspectives we never questioned and assumed as true.

We don't live in a fixed reality; we live in the reflection of our own beliefs. It's a self-made mirror of meaning, and if that mirror is filled with lies, if we are constantly reinforcing separation, blame, and victimhood, then we are living in what can only be described as a personal hell. Not because hell is real, but because we've come to believe in it, to speak from it, to create from it.

When we begin to find purpose in the pattern, when we can see life through the lens of spiritual evolution rather than personal punishment, everything changes. We alter our relationship with Life itself. And when that internal shift occurs, the external world follows, not gradually, exponentially. Simultaneously.

That's the power of the QLT. Not because it adds something new, but because it removes what's false to reveal the truth. It collapses the illusion of separation so that unity can return, and your innate genius can finally express itself fully. When that happens, you don't need a separate coach for your health, your relationships, your money, or your past. Because every issue is connected. Every problem is spiritual at its root. And once you shift at that root level, everything moves.

Unity heals. Gratitude heals. Seeing through the eyes of purpose heals. Because when you find the blessing, the story can end.

And the new one can begin.

Chapter 2: Unconscious Karma Vs. Conscious Co-Creation

You're Always Manifesting, But Are You Aware?

A lot of people talk about "learning how to manifest," as if manifestation is a new skill to be acquired, something you go to a workshop for, or master with enough vision boards and affirmations. But manifestation isn't something we learn; it's something we're already doing. All the time.

You are manifesting every single moment, whether you realize it or not. It isn't optional. It's not a switch you turn on only when you meditate, pray, or visualize. The gift of manifestation, the power of conscious creation, is always on. Even when we don't believe in it. Even when we're using it unconsciously. Even when we're actively speaking words that contradict what the conscious desires.

Manifestation is not about learning how to use the power. It's about remembering you're already using it. Constantly. Relentlessly. Whether or not you desire or choose to.

Here's the core distinction: When we use this gift unconsciously, the results often look like chaos. We call that karma. Cycles repeating. Pain showing up again and again. Life feeling like it's happening to us instead of through us.

But when we use the same gift consciously, when we bring awareness, intention, and alignment into the equation, what emerges is nothing short of miraculous. We begin to witness synchronicities, openings, rapid healing, and quantum shifts that defy logic. But the gift itself didn't change. The source of the creation was always the same.

It's the consciousness behind it that changes the result.

This is what most people have missed up until now. Whether it looks like karma or a miracle, both outcomes are manifestations of the same innate power. The power didn't punish you in one instance and reward you in the other. It simply created from the level of awareness you were vibrating at. It obeyed your instruction, spoken or unspoken, conscious or subconscious.

When people begin to grasp this truth, not just intellectually, but viscerally, they start to carry themselves differently. Reverence replaces recklessness. Words are chosen more carefully. Thoughts are examined. Because once you realize that this power is always running, you stop treating it like a hobby and start honoring it like a sacred responsibility.

You may be familiar with the phrase, "Ask and you shall receive." Most people hear it and think of it as a spiritual cliché. But it's not just spiritual, it's neurological, energetic, and vibrational. Whatever you ask, whether with your words, your energy, or your emotions, you are instructing your reality to respond. You are constantly being answered.

And here's where it gets wild: Your subconscious is the one doing most of the asking. Even when your conscious mind is affirming something lovely, like "I have abundance" or "I'm worthy," if your subconscious is simultaneously broadcasting "Why do I always mess things up?" or "Why does this keep happening to me?" that deeper question is the one the system responds to.

Let's break it down.

Your subconscious mind processes somewhere between 20 million and 400 billion bits of information per second. Yes, *per second*. That's the level of information it's scanning, storing, and patterning from. Your conscious mind, by contrast, can handle anywhere from 40 to 2,000 bits per second. That's like trying to watch a thousand-screen movie with a single pixel. The scale isn't even comparable. The subconscious mind is miraculously fast, a testament to the genius encoded in your very design.

So, what happens when you ask a question like, "Why am I such a screwup?" or "Why is life always so hard?" or "Why can't I get anything right?", your subconscious doesn't judge the question. It doesn't correct you. It simply obeys. It goes out like a cosmic Google search engine and retrieves data to match the inquiry.

And then it floods your consciousness with evidence.

This is why your language matters. Not just what you say out loud, but what you whisper to yourself in moments of frustration. Those unconscious, autopilot questions are still commands. When they come from a place of hate, shame, or blame, they call in more of what you hate. They attract more of what you fear. And your conscious mind, limited and overwhelmed, starts to drown in the emotional residue.

This is where anxiety, worry, doubt, and fear take root. These aren't random emotions. They are chemical consequences, a toxic cocktail of stress hormones and survival signals triggered by unconscious thought loops. When someone lives in this state long enough, it starts to feel normal. But normal isn't the same as natural. The normal state becomes toxic.

The truth is, this emotional loop becomes addictive. That cocktail floods the body repeatedly, reinforcing the same neuronal pathways. The brain starts to fire in the same direction, again and again, until it forgets how to create anything different. That's not lack of ability. That's a manifestation of repetition.

So, let's be clear: You don't have to learn how to manifest; you already are. The question is: Are you aware of what you're creating? Are you aware of the emotional climate that's shaping your next moment? Are you conscious of the energetic commands you're giving the system?

A simple way to preview the next chapter of your life is to take an honest look at how you feel, right now. Because how you feel in this moment is the seed of your next reality. That's not meant to scare you; it's intended to empower you. If you're present enough to feel it, you're powerful enough to shift it.

But to get there, you must look inward to uncover the emotions you've been suppressing and bring them into the light. Not to analyze or judge them, but to feel them. To acknowledge what they've cost you. And most importantly, to discover what they can transform into.

Because here's the secret behind every emotion we perceive as negative: It's carrying a reversal, a hidden invitation to something higher. Anger can become authority and authorship. Shame can become feeling proud and confidence. Fear can become courage. But only if we're willing to feel the emotion without becoming it. We can only do this if we stop running from our feelings and start receiving their messages.

This is the starting point of conscious manifestation. Not from mental scripting or forced positivity, but from full-spectrum awareness. From embodiment. From emotional honesty.

When we learn to live from that place, when our asking comes from wholeness instead of lack, then our life no longer reflects karma; it reflects creation. And the miracles that follow aren't accidents. They are divine. They're inevitable.

Because they were always waiting for you to see what you were really asking for, and for your genius to finally awaken.

From Victim to Creator: Owning What You Hate

There comes a moment in every student's journey when something irreversible begins to happen. The veil lifts, even slightly, and they start to realize that everything in their life, every situation, every repeated pattern, every stuck point or miracle, has been co-created. Not just the good stuff. Not just the breakthroughs or answered prayers, all of it. Every experience was shaped by either a conscious or unconscious decree.

And when this realization truly lands, it doesn't feel gentle. It doesn't arrive with soothing background music and angelic lights. It often comes with grief. Shock. Sometimes anger. Sometimes shame. Because what they begin to see is that they weren't victims of circumstance: Even when they didn't know it, even when they didn't want to be, they were participants in creation.

To move from unconscious to conscious creation demands something fierce. It requires courage, the kind of courage that shatters denial and pierces through decades of identity. It also requires accountability, not the shame-based version that punishes the self, but the sacred kind that says, "If I created this, I can transform it. If I built this reality, I can make a new one."

For most, the shift doesn't happen because they're spiritually enlightened or awake enough to float into a new level of awareness. It happens because they're finally in enough pain to surrender. Pain becomes the invitation. The sharp edge of contrast that makes their current way of being unbearable. And when the ache gets loud enough, they become willing to try something radical, something that often stands in direct opposition to what they've been taught, or conditioned to believe, or clung to for decades.

This is where courage really comes in.

It takes immense bravery to lay down the identity you've been wearing for most of your life, especially when that identity isn't just yours, but was handed down. Often, what we call "self" is actually a collection of inherited perspectives, emotional postures, and subconscious conclusions absorbed from generations before us. You don't have to look very far to see it. It is right inside of you and in front of your face.

A child grows up in a home where money is always scarce, or trust is always broken, or emotions are always suppressed. Maybe that child rebels. Swears they'll never be like their parents. Builds a life that looks completely different on the outside. But even in that rebellion, if they haven't examined the being underneath their actions, they're still manifesting from the same emotional residue.

Because it's not what we do that shapes our life. It's who we're being behind the doing.

Our actions are just expressions of our state of being. And if that state is soaked in fear, anger, or resentment, then no matter how hard we try to change our circumstances, we end up re-creating the same energy in new forms. Different job, same story. New relationship, same arguments. Healthier lifestyle, same self-sabotage. The costumes change, but the cast remains the same.

That's why so many people spend years doing personal growth work, reading books, attending seminars, practicing tools, and still feel stuck. They've changed their habits, but not their frequency. They're still creating from the being of a victim, or the being of someone who resents the world, or the being of someone constantly proving they're not broken.

And the system always matches the signal.

The system is always honest. It will never betray the frequency you're living from. And if that frequency is unresolved pain, it won't just echo in your circumstances; it will echo in your body.

The more someone carries unprocessed anger, suppressed resentment, or silent frustration, the more their body becomes the mirror. These emotions don't just live in the psyche. They settle into the cells. They begin to shape physiology. Tensions form. Inflammation builds. Energy stops flowing.

The liver, the gallbladder, the tendons and ligaments, the skeletal structure, each of these can be impacted by the emotional signals the body has been asked to store. High blood pressure, chronic muscle pain, digestive disorders, brittle bones, and joint degeneration are often seen as "diseases," but many are actually side effects of living in a long-term emotional prison. The body becomes a map of the beliefs we have yet to update.

What we call illness is often a message. A cry for coherence. A signal that we're out of alignment with our own truth.

And what is that misalignment rooted in? Separation.

Separation from self. Separation from Life. Separation from God.

That's what victimhood really is: not a personality trait, but a symptom of forgetting who you are. A forgetting that says, "Life is happening to me, and I have no power here." But it's a lie. And like all lies, it creates suffering.

Hell is not a destination. It's not an afterlife punishment. It's a state of being. A way of living that's disconnected from Source. A belief system in which love feels far away, and power feels unreachable. A reality made of conclusions that were never questioned, and of inherited pain that was never transmuted.

But once you realize that the hell you're living in is not a curse, it's a reflection, you're no longer bound by it.

You can begin to shift. You can start to see that your suffering wasn't proof that life is cruel. It was proof that you were ready to remember your power. Instead of being reclaimed by trauma, you can be reclaimed by truth. Fear is replaced by love.

And when that shift happens, the body follows. The genius within you, once dormant, begins to stir. The cells remember. The nervous system calms. The story starts to change.

Not because you forced it. But because you owned what you hated. And in that ownership, you found your way back home. The home that was always inside you and forever will be!

The True Miracle

So many people spend their lives searching for a miracle. They chase it like it's a rare event, a prize reserved for the worthy, the desperate, or the spiritually elite. But what they have yet to realize is that the miracle isn't missing. It's misidentified.

Life itself is the miracle.

Every breath, every moment, every tear shed in silence, every sunrise taken for granted, all of it is miraculous. And because life is a miracle, everything within it is, too. There's no separation, no category labeled "ordinary" and another "divine." It's *all* divine. The sacred isn't something we visit. It's something we live in. It's something we are.

But when we live inside the paradigm of right and wrong, when we filter our experiences through judgment, our vision becomes distorted. We can no longer see the miracle because we're too busy labeling what's good and what's bad. We miss the wonder because we've become the judge. Anger, resentment, hatred, shame, blame, and guilt aren't just emotional weights; they are filters. They dull our perception and close our eyes to the true nature of life.

The miracle doesn't disappear. We just stop being able to see it.

As soon as we begin taking accountability for our emotions, our pain, our patterns, and our projections, we start to exit the duality. Instead of living in a reactive fight-or-flight loop, bouncing between good and bad, right and wrong, we step into a new posture. One of reverence. One of awareness. One of stillness.

This is the beginning of becoming an objective observer.

And when awareness is coupled with this kind of observation, a sacred noticing without judgment, the power of conscious co-creation begins to reveal itself. Not as a concept, but as a lived experience.

The shift doesn't usually happen overnight. At first, a person begins to feel the pain of the old lens, the ache of constantly judging themselves, others, life. They realize how much energy it takes to live in that divided place. They begin to sense that the suffering they've called normal isn't truth, it's distortion. And in that recognition, something breaks open. They begin to crave a new way of seeing. They begin to remember truth.

But here's the thing: That new lens doesn't become available merely because they want it. In fact, the very word "want" means to desire, but NOT have. It only becomes accessible when they're willing to turn inward, when they begin to acknowledge and actually feel the emotions they've spent a lifetime marking as wrong. Then they can make a new choice.

If someone believes anger is wrong, all they'll see in the world is more anger. More threat. More things to judge, suppress, or avoid. But when they stop judging the anger, when they allow themselves to observe it without flinching, they begin to reclaim their power as the creator of their own experience.

This is where the miracle reappears, and the miracle comes from within the person.

Most people talk about actions and consequences, as if life is some kind of moral scoreboard. But consequence still carries the charge of judgment. It sounds like punishment. Like something you deserve for doing something wrong. And as long as the lens of "deserve" is present, the person remains stuck in right-versus-wrong thinking.

But when a person shifts into seeing actions and results, neutral, nonjudgmental, observable reality, they begin to access a deeper intelligence. It's no longer about blame. It's about feedback. Cause and effect. Creation and reflection.

And something extraordinary happens inside the brain when this shift takes place.

The moment the individual steps out of judgment and into observation, the chemistry of the brain begins to change. The pituitary gland, sometimes called the master gland, releases compounds associated with wisdom and intuitive insight. These aren't metaphors. They're measurable shifts in biochemistry. The brain is a dynamic, living system, and slight changes in internal chemistry can alter perception in profound ways.

Think of the brain as a circuit board. If the internal "water" it runs through is too distilled, if there are no minerals, no conductors, it can't carry current. But the moment you add even a trace of mineral back into that water, it begins to conduct again. Electricity flows. Information moves. Insight returns.

The same principle applies here. The moment we stop bathing the brain in the chemicals of fear, stress, and separation, and instead create the conditions for ease, the system lights up. A person begins to think clearly. Perceive truthfully. Feel deeply. And, most importantly, create intentionally.

Because for the higher brain to function, it requires the body to exit the survival state.

This means the nervous system shifts from sympathetic fight-or-flight into parasympathetic ease and regulation; the greater the ease, the greater the access to intuition, clarity, and wisdom. And when that shift occurs, the individual doesn't just feel better. They perceive a different world entirely.

It's not that the world changed. It's that they changed frequency.

All things are frequency, every thought, emotion, word, and cell. And when the chemical frequency of the body shifts, a new channel becomes available. Like tuning a radio dial, we move from static to music, from noise to signal. And on that channel, the miracle was always playing. We just couldn't hear it until we changed our frequency.

This is the real miracle.

Not something outside of nature, but the full embrace of it. Not a moment of magic, but a life lived in coherence. When you stop seeing life through the wounded observer and begin witnessing it through the eyes of the objective observer, you know what was always there:

Nothing is separate. Nothing is wasted. Nothing is missing.

Everything is connected. Everything is a blessing. Everyone is whole when they remember.

The miracle is not in the event. It's in the awareness of the event.

It's in waking up to the truth that life has always been for you. Every loss. Every moment. Every emotion you were taught to hate. It all belongs.

And once you see it clearly, you stop needing a miracle.

Because you realize you are a miracle, a genius designed for creation.

Chapter 3: Becoming a Master of Your Patterns

Instead of Releasing, Study and Transform the Pattern

Most personal development modalities will tell you to let it go. To release your anger. To get rid of it. You've heard the phrases: Move on. Breathe it out. Set it down. Forgive and forget. But here's the thing nobody stops to question: What does "release" actually mean?

To release. As in, to rent again.

Think about that. The root of the word "release" implies a cycle, not a liberation. It suggests you're giving something up temporarily, not owning it fully. You're disowning it without understanding it. And what we disown will circle back, every time. Like an unpaid bill, it doesn't disappear. It collects interest. It keeps costing you, emotionally, financially, physically, even if you've convinced yourself you're done with it.

So, in this work, we don't teach people to "release" their patterns. We teach them to study them. To own them. To get intimate with them. To earn a metaphorical PhD in their emotional landscape.

When I say, "get a PhD," I mean know the terrain. Know the telltale signs of when a pattern is about to hijack your system. Recognize the sensations, the tone of voice you slip into, the posture, the shutdown, the speed of breath, the tightness in your chest, the narrative that creeps back in. These are your clues. This is your curriculum.

Let's take anger as an example. I'm sure at some point in your life, you've been consumed by it. Maybe you exploded and said things you regretted. Or perhaps you did the opposite, went silent, withdrew, swallowed it down, only to burn up inside. Both are expressions of the same energy. And both usually lead to the same result: disconnection. When you're operating from this place, you're not taking aligned action. You're reacting from fight or flight. You're not in your center. You're not in your power.

That's why most emotional reactivity doesn't lead to resolution. It leads to repetition.

So, what do we do instead?

Step one: Own it. If you deny a feeling, that feeling will own you. It will control your thoughts, drive your decisions, shape your relationships. You may think you're in charge, but the emotion will be behind the wheel.

Step two: Make it okay. Stop demonizing your humanity. Whatever you're feeling is valid. You're not broken because you're angry. You're not wrong for feeling grief, fear, jealousy, rage. These emotions are not a moral failing; they are part of your nervous system.

Step three: Trace it. Ask yourself, When did I first feel this way? And more importantly, What did I believe about life when I did? Usually, the original wound is wrapped in "not" statements. *Life's not fair. I'm not good enough. I shouldn't have to go through this. My parents weren't supposed to be that way. I shouldn't feel this broken.* These thoughts become emotional contracts. And you've been renewing those contracts unconsciously for years.

Once you begin identifying the pattern, it's time to observe its trajectory. When does it show up? What's the trigger? What do you do next? What results does it create? What does it cost you?

And be honest here. The cost isn't theoretical. It's tangible.

What has this pattern cost you in your life?

Has it cost you intimacy? Financial opportunity? Peace of mind? Creativity? Joy? Sleep? Confidence?

For most people, the answer is all of the above.

But if a pattern costs you something, it must be giving you something, too.

And this is where it gets uncomfortable, because the payoff is rarely what we think we desire. But it's what our nervous system believes we require.

So, ask yourself: What do I get to have when I keep this pattern alive?

Maybe you get to be right. Perhaps you get to blame someone else. Perhaps you get to avoid failure by never fully trying. Perhaps you get to hold on to a story that makes you feel secure.

Why would being right be such a seductive payoff? Because there's a massive energetic hit that comes with it. I'm not talking about morality. I'm talking about chemistry. When you feel self-righteous, when you believe with full conviction that it's their fault, that you're the one who knows the truth, it creates a neurochemical fix.

And I use the word "fix" here intentionally. Like a drug hit. Because that's precisely what it is.

Your body is a chemical factory. And emotions are biochemical signals. When you activate resentment, judgment, blame, or superiority, your body produces specific compounds. And the more often you experience them, the more your body becomes dependent on them. It's no different than becoming addicted to sugar, alcohol, or nicotine. Except this addiction hides behind the mask of your personality. It sounds like your voice. It feels like your truth.

But it's not truth. It's a loop.

And until you study the loop, understand the reward it's giving you, the chemistry it's feeding, the story it's reinforcing, you won't be able to shift it.

Once you start to really see the pattern, movement becomes possible. The energy trapped inside the emotion can begin to transform. Not because you forced it out. But because you finally brought it into the light.

There are countless practices and exercises that can accelerate this movement. Most of them involve not force or logic, but love. Love is the alchemy. Love is the antidote. Love is what unravels the knot from the inside out.

But love isn't always soft. Sometimes love looks like radical honesty. Like sitting still with your pain instead of fixing it. Like choosing accountability over blame. Like letting your heart break open so something new can be born.

So don't rush to release your patterns. Don't try to bypass the lesson. Don't just exhale it away.

Study it. Own it. Honor it.

And then, when it's ready to move, it will.

Because what we study with love, transforms.

From Reaction to Mastery

As you move deeper into your "PhD" discovery process, into the honest, often painful study of your patterns, something begins to emerge. You start to notice the recurrence. Not just of the pattern itself, but of the emotional loops, the thoughts that tag along, the energy that seems to rise before you even realize what triggered it. It's like déjà vu with a darker flavor. You've been here before, many times. And unless you understand how that pattern actually functions, how it's wired into your system, it will not only continue, but it will strengthen over time.

Why?

Because the more frequently a pattern runs, the more your nervous system begins to believe it is you. The anger, the avoidance, the self-sabotage, the excuses, all of it becomes woven into your perceived identity. It becomes part of your "I am." *I'm just someone who can't trust people. I've always been this way. Life's always been hard for me.*

And the moment you identify with a pattern, it becomes challenging to disrupt. Because now, it's not just something happening to you. It's something you believe you are.

That belief system, no matter how painful, is familiar. And the emotions attached to it begin to function like a drug. I mean that literally. The chemicals your body produces during episodes of judgment, blame, shame, resentment, and self-righteousness give you a hit. Just like cocaine gives a hit. It doesn't matter whether those chemicals feel good or bad; your body craves them because they're familiar. Predictable. Stabilizing, in a strange way. Even suffering has its own twisted kind of comfort when it's what you know best.

But just like someone in the grip of addiction, most people can't see how the very substance they're hooked on is eroding their potential. The person on cocaine might deny its effects, even as their life crumbles. And the same is true of these internally produced drugs, the ones generated by emotional loops and mental constructs.

Most people have yet to realize how those chemicals are affecting their higher brain function. How the persistent repetition of an unchallenged belief is keeping them locked in survival mode. How it's keeping them from feeling love, receiving insight, experiencing peace. Until they have had enough pain, they often remain asleep in their addiction.

Here's the truth that changes everything: The limiting pattern will stay in place until the person has an experience that directly contradicts the belief at its core.

Let's say someone has spent their whole life believing that money only comes through struggle. That you have to grind, sacrifice, and push just to survive. That abundance is something "other people" get to have. That belief, if left unchallenged, will continue manifesting as exhaustion, undercharging, scarcity, and resentment.

But then, something happens. Maybe through this work, or a new choice, or a moment of grace, they suddenly experience ease. They make money without stress. They receive a gift. An opportunity lands effortlessly.

And for a brief moment, their nervous system gets to feel what's possible outside the old story.

That moment is gold.

It's the crack in the armor, the opening in the matrix. But for the shift to become sustainable, they can't just feel it and move on. They have an opportunity. They get to study it. Speak it. Integrate it.

Because only when a person can clearly identify what changed, internally, to create the new external experience, can they begin to rebuild their trust. Trust in themselves. Trust in Life. Trust in the sacred, astonishing truth of co-creation.

That's when something begins to rewire.

The greater they name the shift, the more they stabilize it. The greater they stabilize it, the more they start to expect miracles instead of chasing them. Their manifestations become bolder. Their actions become cleaner. Their timelines compress. What used to take five years now takes five weeks. What felt impossible suddenly feels inevitable.

But here's something important to understand. Right before a new expansion, right before the breakthrough, there's almost always a constriction.

It might show up as anxiety. Resistance. Confusion. Fatigue. Or even a temporary regression into old behavior. But this constriction isn't a sign that you're going backward. It's a birth canal.

It's the final compression that precedes new life.

Just as a seed breaks before it sprouts. Just the way a breath catches before a sob. Just like darkness feels thickest right before the dawn breaks, your system is reorganizing itself to accommodate a bigger, brighter version of you. And that constriction isn't punishment. It's preparation.

Most people retreat at this point. They misread the tightening. They assume they're doing something wrong. But if you can stay present during this contraction, if you can observe it without collapsing into it, you'll begin to see it for what it really is:

The opening.

Every expansion requires an inner death. A shedding. A transforming, not of the feeling, but of the identity attached to the old frequency. And the only way to move through it is with awareness, humility, and a deep commitment to presence and ease.

You are becoming someone new.

Not by changing who you are, but by remembering who you were before the pattern took hold.

So, study the recurrence. Don't fear it. Don't bypass it.

Let it teach you. Let it show you the truth you're now ready to receive.

And when you finally meet the old pattern with a new choice, again and again, you move from reactivity to mastery.

You stop surviving your life.

And you start creating it.

Living in Ease

The ultimate result of inner alignment is not perfection. It's not the disappearance of pain or the absence of triggers. It's ease.

And ease, contrary to popular belief, is not passive. It's not doing nothing. It's not bypassing discomfort. Ease is what arises when a person learns how to move *with* life instead of fighting against it. And this kind of ease is remembered.

As someone goes through this process, this deep work of owning, observing, and transmuting their patterns, the pain doesn't vanish. The contractions still come. The emotional resistance can still tighten. But over time, they begin to recognize the contraction for what it really is: a gateway, a portal to the next level of expansion.

Just like going to the gym.

Let's be real. Most people don't love dragging themselves into a gym, especially not in the beginning. That inner voice kicks up: Do we really have to do this today? Maybe we can skip just this once. But if they stick with it, if they show up, sweat it out, stay in it, something shifts. The resistance softens. The body opens. And by the time they finish the workout, they feel incredible. Not just physically, but emotionally, even spiritually. There's clarity. Pride. Strength. Lightness.

They may have dreaded the effort, but they love the after.

That's the alchemy of committed practice. And that's what begins to happen on the inner journey, too.

At first, it feels like pushing through molasses. You don't want to feel the grief. You don't want to own the anger. You don't want to sit with the fear that has been buried under performance, people-pleasing, or perfectionism. But as you begin to feel it, really feel it, your internal chemistry starts to change.

Your inner drug factory, the one that's been pumping out cortisol, adrenaline, and a cocktail of emotional stress hormones, begins to shift production. Instead of sadness, doubt, and anxiety, the system starts to produce gratitude. Appreciation. Reverence. Peace. Even playfulness.

And here's the beautiful irony: Those chemicals aren't being produced because you got what you desired; they're being made because you finally stopped running from what you felt.

The act of showing up for yourself, especially when it feels hard, starts to rewire your emotional reward system. You no longer need chaos or crisis to initiate growth. Instead of avoidance, you begin to seek it from a place of desire and choice.

Much like someone with a sports injury who begins physical therapy, their pain is unbearable in the beginning. They'll do whatever it takes just to stop hurting. The rehab is grueling, stretching through scar tissue and rebuilding strength in weakened muscles. Every movement feels like a mountain. But day by day, something shifts. The pain lessens, the mobility returns. The strength rebuilds.

And at some point, they're no longer showing up to escape pain.

They're showing up to expand possibilities.

That's the turning point.

Personal growth is no longer about fixing what's broken. It becomes about reclaiming what's whole. About increasing strength, flexibility, vitality. Emotional flexibility. Energetic strength. Spiritual resilience.

You begin to choose growth not because you have to, but because you love the new you being revealed. Not because you're trying to outrun suffering, but because you love remembering your highest expression.

This is the shift that turns healing into empowerment and transforms your life raft of inner work into a lifestyle. You no longer track your life by what you're letting go of; you begin to measure it by what's being transformed and returning to you.

The joy is returning. The clarity is returning, too. The confidence, the creativity, the connection, they all begin to come home to you.

And when you shift your focus from releasing to receiving, from pain avoidance to the return of wholeness, your entire system gets a new instruction. That instruction is no longer "Something's wrong with me." It becomes "Something beautiful is on its way."

This mindset becomes a supercharger. It accelerates growth not through force, but through alignment.

Because when you stop trying to escape discomfort and start honoring the strength you're reclaiming, ease begins to flow.

And that ease is not a reward. It's not a finish line.

It's the natural state that was buried beneath the fight.

It was always yours.

You just made a choice to explore and meet yourself honestly and sincerely to remember.

Chapter 4: Language Shapes Reality

Words as Portals

Henry Ford once said, "Whether you think you can, or you think you can't, you're right." At first glance, it reads like a simple motivational quote. But sit with it longer, and you begin to understand that it's not just about attitude; it's about reality: how it forms, how it bends, and how it obeys the direction of your words.

Across the spectrum of human history and consciousness studies, from sacred scripture to personal growth seminars to quantum physics textbooks, a common thread weaves through them all: Language creates. Words are not just descriptors of experience; they generate it. They are creative instruments that carry frequency. And frequency, as science and spirit both agree, forms the building blocks of matter.

Every word we speak is a spell we cast. A prayer we utter. A vibration we send into the field. The God I speak of here is not the man in the sky with a beard and a gavel, but the quantum mirror, the divine intelligence that simply reflects back whatever we project into it. If we speak limitations, it reflects them. If we talk about possibilities, it expands them. If we declare that life is unfair, we will inevitably encounter more evidence to prove it true.

This is not positive thinking. This is not woo-woo wishful philosophy. This is resonance. Physics. Cause and effect. We live inside a divine amusement park that gives us more of whatever ride we get in line for. And the ticket? The words we say, especially the ones we say when we're not paying attention.

This co-creative power doesn't start working when we become aware of it; it's been running all along. Like a faucet left on in the background, it's constantly pouring into our lives, matching the temperatures of our thoughts, tone, and unconscious beliefs. Whether you're in peace or panic, joy or despair, the mirror never turns off.

Scripture refers to this as the principle of sowing and reaping. What you plant in thought, you harvest in reality. But it's not just about what you consciously intend; it's about the subtle undercurrent. If your inner language is laced with anger, fear, blame, or resentment, that becomes the compost for your next reality. Speak shame, get shame. Speak unworthiness, and you will gather more proof of your unworthiness. The system is generous, but it is not selective. It responds to whatever frequency is dominant, especially the ones you're most familiar with.

For many who've walked through trauma, this becomes a painful loop. One of the hardest things to receive, when your body has been in fight-or-flight mode for years, is genuine appreciation. Not because others aren't offering it, but because your nervous system has no receptor for it. Gratitude feels foreign. Secure feels suspicious. So, when someone says something kind, "You did a great job on that project," the reflex is to deflect. "It was nothing," they shrug. It seems casual, but it's not. That phrase is a shield. A spell. A quiet, unconscious way of saying: *I don't believe I'm worthy of praise, so I'll push it away before it exposes my discomfort.*

Trauma alters language, but more importantly, language reinforces trauma. When someone has been conditioned to believe they are unworthy, unseen, or unappreciated, their words follow suit. Their inner dialogue becomes a battleground, and eventually, the body becomes a part of the war.

I've seen this in people who live with chronic pain or autoimmune conditions. The body is attacking itself. Not because it is broken, but because the person's inner language is soaked in self-attack. You can't berate yourself all day and expect your cells to feel secure. The body listens to the frequency beneath the words. It obeys the tone of the narrator. If the narrator is cruel, critical, or collapsing, the immune system responds accordingly.

Even small interactions can reveal the language loops we're stuck in. Imagine someone saying to their spouse, "Hey, could you put the cap on the toothpaste?" A simple request. But the response? "I can never do anything right for you." That sentence is not really about toothpaste. It's about a lifetime of inner dialogue suddenly echoing out loud.

In that moment, what's being triggered isn't just the conversation, it's the shame script that's been running for years. The voice that says, "You're always wrong. You're always messing it up. You're not enough." That voice is ancient, internal, and relentless. And when it hears a new input that even vaguely resembles it, it flares up in defense. The person isn't reacting to you; they're reacting to themselves through you.

That's the thing about being triggered: The more we hate the voice in our head, the louder we fight when someone else accidentally mirrors it. Most people don't realize how many voices are inside of them until one of them gets poked. The louder the reaction, the more it reveals. And behind every overreaction is usually a deep, unhealed conversation happening within.

We all walk around inside our language field. We bathe in it. We breathe it in like air. And unless we become aware of the words we're speaking, thinking, or absorbing, we will live inside realities we never chose, realities built by inherited phrases, generational beliefs, and trauma-soaked vocabularies.

But language is not just a cage. It is a portal. A bridge. A seed.

And the moment we choose to speak something different, not just perform positivity, but speak from a truer, cleaner place within us, we begin to change not just what we experience, but what we expect.

The voice of God in your life may not sound like thunder from the clouds; it may sound like the words you whisper when no one is listening.

And the most radical shift might begin the moment you finally say, "I am worthy of peace. I am open to love. I am secure now."

Not to perform for the mirror.

But to become what you've always been.

The Shift from Processing to Outcomes

There's a profound difference between processing and outcomes, though many people unconsciously blur the line. Most people assume that outcomes refer to results, things in the physical world that they can point to. A new car. A better job. A romantic partner. A house with more light. And on the surface, yes, those are results. But what makes them feel like outcomes to the human nervous system is not the thing itself; it's what we believe those things will produce inside of us.

Most people chase results not for the result, but for a feeling they hope the result will finally give them. Maybe when the business succeeds, they'll finally feel proud of themselves. Maybe when they find the perfect partner, they'll finally feel chosen. Maybe when the bank account hits that number, they'll finally feel secure.

They believe the outside world must shift for their inner world to find peace. That's the spell of misdirected manifestation: doing something physical to feel something emotional. But it's backwards.

When someone lives this way, they can accumulate all the outer trophies: The six-figure job. The loving spouse. The smiling kids. The gorgeous home. And still, nothing silences the internal narrative that drove them to chase it all in the first place.

They might be building a life out of resentment, out of spite, out of the desperate hunger to prove something to someone who never saw them, maybe a parent who said, "You'll never amount to anything." And no matter how many accolades they stack in the 3D world, if they're still carrying that voice, the one that whispers *you're not enough*, they will never fully feel the success they've created. The outcomes remain hollow, like decorating an empty house and wondering why it still feels cold.

Because real outcomes begin in the body, they start with how you feel before any visualizations, intentions, or declarations are spoken into the mirror of reality. When you shift into the energy of already being, already being enough, being secure, already being loved, the body releases. The nervous system softens. You drop out of fight or flight and into rest, receptivity, and resonance.

And then, something sacred happens: The vision arrives, not from grasping or mental effort, but from an inner place of clarity. The vision isn't something you try to conjure up; it's something that reveals itself. You don't force it into being. You receive it like a memory you had forgotten, something that's always been yours. That's the real meaning of manifestation. It doesn't begin with your mind. It starts with your state.

Our system doesn't visualize first and then relax. It relaxes first, and only then does the truth become visible. The outcome is not something you push into existence; it's something you see more clearly once your body is aligned with peace.

And this kind of seeing doesn't feel like "trying to figure it out." It's not mental gymnastics or strategy sessions with the universe. It's quiet. Gentle. Resonant. Like a tuning fork catching the frequency of something you've always known but never had the words for.

Language reveals exactly where a person is living internally. In many religious traditions, we hear about hell, purgatory, and heaven. But those places are not always future destinations. Often, they're emotional addresses. And our language gives them away.

When someone is stuck in hell, you'll hear it. Their words are soaked in shame and despair. *I'm not good enough. I can't do anything right. I don't know how. I keep trying, but nothing seems to work. Life isn't fair.* Their tone is collapsed. Their inner world is loud and hopeless, and their language echoes the torment they're walking through.

In purgatory, there's motion, but no ground. Most of the sentences end in -ing: I*'m healing. I'm processing. I'm improving. I'm getting better.* It sounds progressive, but listen closely, and you'll notice something is missing: specificity. The person is caught in limbo, where the story is constantly changing but never quite comes to a resolution, where forward motion is discussed, but not deeply felt.

And then, there's heaven. When someone is anchored there, even for a moment, their words shift entirely. They speak from fullness, from love, from direct experience. You'll hear it in the imagery. *I love watching my partner laugh while playing with the kids. I feel so grateful when I walk barefoot on the grass in the morning and hear the birds.* These aren't vague affirmations or ideas. They're vivid. Specific. Alive. You can see what they're saying as they say it. That's not just an emotional connection; that's the pineal gland activating. That's imagination, presence, and gratitude lighting up the system like a symphony.

When someone speaks from that place, they're no longer processing life. They're participating in it. They're not trying to improve. They're in a relationship with the now. And the now becomes fertile ground for outcomes that don't just look good but feel real.

This is the shift, out of mental loops and into embodiment, out of endless processing and into present resonance. Outcomes aren't about what shows up in your life. They're about the state you live in while life unfolds.

If you can feel it first, you won't need to chase it later.

And the outcome, when it arrives, will simply be a mirror of who you've already become.

Speaking From the End: Creating with Outcome-Oriented Words

In scripture, it says that God saw the end from the beginning, and He called it good. Before anything had materialized, before the dust had settled into form or light had split the darkness, it was already good. That's not optimism. That's divine certainty.

Jesus, too, modeled this sacred way of being. When performing miracles, He didn't plead for a result; He gave thanks before the healing had occurred. He blessed the outcome as if it were already here. Because in His knowing, it was.

This is what it means to speak from the end. It's not about pretending. It's about aligning. The language of manifestation doesn't ask for proof. It speaks with assurance, love, and presence as if the thing already exists. Because in a field governed by frequency, it does.

Now, for someone who's experienced deep trauma, this can feel impossible. How do you feel grateful for something you can't yet see? How do you speak with joy about a life that feels so far away?

But here's the key: Co-creation is not something you have to earn. It's already running, whether you're conscious of it or not. Your words, your emotions, and your focus are already participating in the creative process. The invitation is simply to become aware of the gift you've been holding all along.

Gratitude is the activation point. Not gratitude after something arrives, but gratitude before as an expression of trust. And once that thread of appreciation begins to stir in the body, something profound starts to happen. The chemistry shifts. The nervous system softens. The addiction to pain begins to loosen its grip.

For many, that moment of peace, of soft gratitude, is the first time they've felt secure in their own body, not just in their lifetime, but in their entire lineage. The nervous system, once braced against life, starts to exhale. This is the first miracle: The body remembers ease.

So how do we do this? How do we begin to speak from the end?

We speak about the future in the present tense. We stop waiting for permission from the outer world to feel what we desire to feel. Instead, we think and feel it now. Most people unknowingly push their desires away by saying things like, "One day I'll find love," or "When this happens, I'll finally feel happy." But in telling it that way, they keep the outcome at arm's length. They speak as if they're not yet ready, not yet worthy, not yet whole.

But when you speak as if it's already yours, you collapse the timeline. You meet the moment with resonance. The body begins to believe it's secure to have what you've been asking for.

Let's say you're calling in a partner, but you're currently single. Rather than focusing on the absence, you begin to speak as someone who is already in love.

I love how we laugh together in the kitchen. I love holding their hand while we walk through the neighborhood. I love the way I feel secure sharing my truth with them. I love watching them light up when they talk about something they're passionate about.

These aren't affirmations. They're creative declarations. They're acts of emotional rehearsal. And the body doesn't know the difference between memory and imagination. So, as you speak this way, you're not just thinking differently. You're feeling differently. Your cells begin to rearrange. Your chemistry becomes receptive. Your magnetism increases. And soon, the external world starts to match.

But it's not magic. It's responsibility. Because speaking from the end isn't only about calling in what you want, it's about becoming the version of you who lives in that outcome.

Let's say you imagine being with an emotionally safe partner, someone you can share anything with. The question becomes: Are you the kind of person who can hold that kind of intimacy? When conflict arises, do you yell, shut down, or attack? Or do you respond as someone who already trusts love?

You're not just visualizing a dream; you're stepping into a new identity. You're becoming the person that version of life requires. Your words are not just about creation. They are invitations into a different posture, a different nervous system, a different way of being.

And here's the most essential part.

The moment you'll be tested is not when everything is going well. The defining moment always comes in the form of a challenge. It's easy to speak with gratitude when the skies are clear. But when the storm rolls in, that's when you find out if you believe what you've been saying.

Because when you're shifting timelines, the old world will try to pull you back. You'll be tempted to react the way you always have. To spiral into doubt. To collapse into shame. To lash out or shut down.

But if in that moment you pause, breathe, and speak from the heart anyway…

If you can say, I'm secure. I'm chosen. I am loved, right in the middle of fear…

That's when the rewrite begins.

Not just in your mind.

But in your body.

In your field.

And in your future.

Life and Death Are in the Power of the Tongue

As you begin to speak in the way described earlier, with outcome-oriented, love-rooted words, you'll notice that something subtle yet undeniable begins to shift. It won't just be a change in thought or a fleeting mood lift. It will be felt in your body. Tangibly. Physically. As if your cells themselves are listening. Because they are.

Words carry a frequency and have a feeling. And once you start paying attention, you'll notice: Every word you speak invites a sensation. Some words weigh you down. Others lift you. Some flood your body with heat, others with coolness or stillness. Some words activate old survival patterns, leading to a tight chest, clenched jaw, shallow breath. But other words... they tingle.

That tingle, that subtle, shimmering response in your nervous system, is not a coincidence. It's evidence. It's the body's way of saying, *Yes, this is real for us.* This is where life is being welcomed.

To become self-aware in this way is to enter the actual work of language. Not just speaking to be heard but speaking to heal. Speaking to align, speaking to awaken dormant parts of yourself that have been waiting for a voice filled with reverence to call them forward, finally.

You begin to feel this shift in real time. A warmth through your limbs, a buzzing along your spine, a spark that flickers behind your eyes. And it's not just happening in your body; it's also happening in your brain.

Yes, there are literal, biological changes. If someone were to scan your brain before and after a season of intentional speech, weeks or even days of speaking words rooted in love, gratitude, and vision, they would see something miraculous: Areas of the brain that were once dormant begin to glow with activity. Regions that had atrophied from trauma, chronic stress, or emotional neglect begin to light up.

You are not just imagining. You are becoming who you were truly meant to be. You are growing new neural pathways. The tingle in your body is mirrored by the tangle of synapses forming in your brain. You are, in every sense, being renewed.

This is why conditions like Alzheimer's, dementia, and even Parkinson's have been shown to shift in some individuals when the mind and body are reintroduced to meaning, gratitude, imagination, and emotional aliveness. These aren't small things. These are life codes. And when they are spoken, when they are lived, the body responds.

Playfulness returns. Memory improves. Sadness lifts. Not all at once, not always neatly. But undeniably.

Instead of walking through life in a fog of grief, judgment, or resignation, the person begins to experience something sacred: a quiet awe. A renewed reverence. Gratitude that feels cellular, not performative. And it doesn't just shift their mood; it reshapes their entire relationship to Life.

Not just life as in the ticking of time or the biological continuation of days. But Life with a capital L. The eternal essence. The animating presence. The invisible force behind breath, beauty, and being.

When you change your language, you don't just shift your mind. You recalibrate your entire orientation to this Life.

And the moment you speak to Life differently, Life responds in kind.

It begins to show up for you, not as a series of obstacles to overcome, but as a loving presence walking beside you.

Opportunities open. Relationships soften. Your own resistance begins to melt, not because everything outside of you has changed, but because the voice inside of you finally did.

The words you speak aren't just for others to hear.

They are building the world you're living in.

They are sculpting the brain you're thinking with.

They are weaving the frequency your cells are bathing in.

This is why scripture says life and death are in the power of the tongue. Because it's not just poetic metaphor. It's literal, living truth. You speak of life, or you talk about decay. You talk about future, or you reinforce the past. You bless yourself, or you curse your own nervous system.

And every time you speak with love, every time you choose a word that lifts rather than judges, opens rather than closes, you reclaim a little more of your own aliveness.

You don't need perfect language. You don't need polished affirmations. You just need sincerity. Reverence. Presence.

Even now, as you read this, you can feel it. That tingle. That hum. That quiet knowing rising inside your chest.

It's your body remembering what Life feels like.

Don't stop now.

Speak from that place.

Speak to that place.

And watch everything change.

Chapter 5: Feelings First, Thoughts Follow

Why Thought-Based Coaching Falls Short

Most people who come to coaching, even those who appear high functioning, are living with some degree of fight or flight humming beneath the surface. They might not even realize it. It doesn't always look like panic or chaos. Sometimes it shows up as high performance. Achievement. Obsession with growth. But inside, their body is braced. Their breath is shallow. Their nervous system is wired to survive, not to thrive.

And when someone is in a state of survival, asking them to "change their thoughts" is like handing a compass to someone in the middle of a tornado. They can't orient. The sky is spinning too fast. Their internal world is loud, fast, flooded. Thought-based coaching, which often sounds like "Don't think that" or "Just focus on the positive," can become another layer of self-judgment for someone whose inner world already feels like a war zone.

I've been in those rooms, the ones where coaches repeat mantras like: Don't think negative thoughts, stay in a high vibration, be positive, polish your perspective. The problem isn't the intention; it's the approach. The entire coaching model rests on the belief that the mind is the gateway to transformation. But for someone in dysregulation, the mind is the most unstable place to begin.

When someone's thoughts are spiraling, their system is not asking for strategy, it is asking for security. Trying to think better thoughts from that state only adds fuel to the fire. Now they're not just suffering, they're also failing at "being spiritual."

What most thought-based coaching does, without meaning to, is keep the person in their head. It keeps them analyzing, processing, spinning in the question: Am I thinking the right thing? Am I doing this right? Why am I still stuck?

This hyper-monitoring only strengthens the inner critic. The internal dialogue becomes louder, not quieter. The body tightens. The breath disappears. And despite all the effort, the person feels more disconnected than when they started.

Even when people bring in meditation to calm the mind, it often takes hours, or even weeks, of consistent practice to quiet the noise. And for some, the pressure to "clear your mind" becomes another impossible standard. They sit down to meditate, but instead of finding peace, they're swarmed by a thousand voices. And they think that means they're broken.

But they're not broken. They're activated.

And in an activated state, the work is not to control the thoughts.

It's to calm the body.

One of my mentors once said, "Anything other than your highest choice contains elements of self-sabotage." That landed in me like a bell, because it reframed the whole game. It's not about trying to fix every fear-based thought. It's about tuning into the frequency that allows the highest choice to even become visible.

Imagine you have this magnificent, miraculous power to create, to design your life, moment by moment, in collaboration with the divine. And then one day, instead of stepping into that power, you say, "You know what? I think I'll go with my 2,487th-highest choice today, the one that's a little safer, a little smaller, a little more familiar."

Why? Because the nervous system didn't feel secure enough to reach higher.

Because somewhere inside, the body was still rehearsing an old memory. An old pain. A belief that it wasn't secure to be powerful. A belief that said *This is too good to last* or *You always mess things up.*

When a person has been living in survival mode for a long time, the mind becomes slippery. Focus feels impossible. The past keeps flooding the present. Old emotions rise without warning. Trying to "control your thoughts" in that state is like trying to put out a wildfire with a squirt gun.

And yet, people ask, *How do I stop thinking this way? How do I change my thoughts?* But "how" is the trap. The moment you ask how, you're back in the mind. You've just been pulled out of the body, out of the now, and into another cycle of searching.

There is a more straightforward way.

You start with the body.

You start by shifting out of the sympathetic nervous system, the state of fight, flight, or freeze, and into the parasympathetic, the state of rest, digest, receive. You start with breath. With sensation. With stillness. You let the body know: You're safe and secure now.

And once the body softens, once there's enough ease in the system to allow presence, only then do the thoughts begin to quiet on their own. Not because you wrestled them into silence, but because they simply no longer match your frequency.

The deeper the ease, the faster the breakthrough.

But that's not what most of us were taught. We were trained in the opposite direction.

In school, we were rewarded for how well we could memorize facts. Repeat information. Perform knowledge. Our education system taught us to worship the intellect and dismiss the body. We became brilliant at regurgitation and empty at embodiment.

This is what I call mental masturbation. It's the looping of intellect with no anchoring in wisdom. It keeps people stuck in a 3D survival-based world, mistaking mental effort for real growth.

But to use the gift of co-creation consciously, we migrate out of that paradigm. We get to move from 3D into the realms of 4D and 5D consciousness.

In 4D, a person begins to see that the outer world is a mirror of their inner world. They stop chasing the illusion of control and start noticing how their thoughts, words, and especially their feelings are shaping the world around them. This is the realm of awakening.

In 5D, they move beyond even that. They begin to see that everything, every experience, every person, every emotion, is an expression of love. They don't focus on what they want to manifest to feel good. They feel good first. They feel love. Gratitude. Peace. And then, whatever exists at that frequency naturally reveals itself.

This is the opposite of mental visualizing.

This is embodiment. Resonance. Presence.

And this is why thought-based coaching, while helpful for the mind, will always fall short if it doesn't honor the deeper intelligence of the body and the nervous system.

Because thoughts don't lead feeling.

Feeling leads thought.

And once you feel different, the thoughts will follow like loyal soldiers, walking in the direction your body has already decided to go.

Feelings Are 80% Manifestation

Have you ever done affirmations? Most people have, at some point, whether they wrote them on sticky notes or repeated them in the mirror with hope in their voices and doubt in their chests. And yet, for many, the results feel... flat. Like shouting into a canyon and only hearing your own emptiness echo back.

If you've been doing affirmations with little to no change in your reality, it's not because you're broken. It's because your feelings haven't aligned with what you're saying. You can declare, "I am wealthy," but if your body is tight with stress over bills, if you're holding your breath when you open your bank account, if your nervous system is still running the story of "There's never enough," then the words don't land. They don't root. They don't grow.

In fact, the more you say the affirmation from a place of internal contradiction, the more likely you are to notice things that intensify your emotional dissonance. Suddenly, the bill is higher than expected. The job opportunity falls through. The unexpected expense hits. Not because the universe is cruel, but because your dominant frequency, your felt experience, is what's being matched. Not your words.

Words carry power, but feeling is the engine behind the spell. The tone. The vibration. The charge. That's what moves the world.

Take a word like "fuck," for example. Some people hate it. Others use it like punctuation. But beyond the cultural judgments, it reveals something profound about language and emotion. That one word, depending on how it's said, can mean a thousand different things.

You can say it in anger and cut someone to the core. You can say it in joy and ignite laughter across a room. You can whisper it in intimacy, scream it in frustration, laugh it in surprise.

It's not the word. It's the feeling riding beneath it.

And the same is true of every word you speak.

Feeling transmutes meaning. It is the architect behind creation. And for someone who has spent years in fight or flight, the ability to consciously generate feeling, on command, in the direction of love, is not always easy. In fact, it can feel impossible at first.

That's because survival mode hijacks the emotional body. It keeps you reacting to whatever is happening, rather than responding from your center. Instead of being the conscious creator of your inner state, you become the victim of it, chased by the past, braced against the future.

But the moment you step into emotional self-mastery, everything begins to shift. The moment you realize that how you feel is the signal, that your emotional state is 80% of your manifestation field, you start to reclaim the steering wheel.

The greater your capacity to regulate your inner chemistry, the greater your ability to hold a powerful frequency, even in the face of challenge. And the more grounded your internal frequency becomes, the more naturally life aligns around you.

Responsibility, clarity, and influence are drawn to those who are emotionally anchored.

And yes, the universe absolutely responds to that level of coherence.

Responsibilities are not burdens. They are reflections of your level of mastery. They arrive when you are ready. They stretch you, refine you, elevate you. And they flow directly from your ability to maintain inner congruence, not perfection, but presence.

Because your divine being, your truest self, is already whole. Already radiant. Already worthy. Trauma, however, acts like a film over that light. A filter. A distortion that convinces you that *you* are the filter. That your wounds define your worth. That the pain is more real than the love beneath it.

But it's not true.

The being underneath has never been touched by the trauma. It has only been hidden by it.

This reminds me of a quote from the Gospel of Thomas: "If you bring forth what is within you, what is within you will save you. If you do not bring forth what is within you, what is within you will destroy you."

What does that mean?

It means that what you bury inside you doesn't die. It grows. It festers. It becomes the silent architect of your reality. The suppressed feelings, the unspoken truths, the ungrieved losses don't disappear. They calcify. And eventually, they speak louder than your affirmations.

If you don't go within, you end up living inside the prison of your avoidance.

People don't get bitter because they're evil. They get bitter because they've spent decades building a life around unprocessed wounds. And the more real those wounds feel, the more defended they become. Until eventually, the false self, the one built from pain, shame, and fear, becomes more familiar than the soul underneath.

But here's the miracle.

When someone finds the courage to turn toward what they've been running from, something sacred happens.

When they finally stop trying to bypass the pain, when they allow themselves to feel, not as a victim, but as a seeker, they begin to unearth the truth beneath the trauma.

And what they find is not devastation.

It's God.

It's Love.

It's Truth.

Because the truth doesn't shame you. The truth doesn't beat you. The truth frees you.

The truth reminds you that your beingness was never damaged.

Only covered.

And when you uncover it, when you speak to it, feel it, live from it, your manifestations become reflections of your wholeness, not your wounds.

So, the next time you say an affirmation, ask yourself:

Am I saying this from alignment?

Or am I saying this to escape how I really feel?

Because if you can begin to feel what you desire to become, if you can anchor into the emotional frequency of love, gratitude, and inner peace before the outcome arrives, then the outcome won't matter.

You'll already be free.

And that is the tangible manifestation.

Emotion as Chemistry: The Frequency of Transformation

What we often label as emotion, joy, grief, anger, shame, is, at its core, chemistry. A feeling is not just a story in your head. It is a chemical reaction, a biochemical signature released into your bloodstream. And your body, brilliant and ancient, is the factory that produces every drop of it.

Your body is not just a vessel. It is a living, breathing pharmacy. A sacred, responsive laboratory that produces these emotional compounds based on the instructions it receives: your thoughts, your environment, your memories, your language, your breath.

Every feeling you experience carries its own chemical formula. And those formulas either support your vitality or begin to poison it slowly.

If you consistently produce the chemistry of anxiety, for example, tightness in the chest, cortisol in the blood, breath stuck in the upper lungs, then your body becomes conditioned to that cocktail. It learns to live in it. Eventually, it starts to crave it, even though it's toxic.

And when that happens, your system is no longer filtering toxins efficiently. The liver, the immune system, the gut all get bogged down. Over time, you can't release what you're bringing in. So, your body becomes inflamed, exhausted, confused. Not because something outside of you is broken, but because you've been trapped in the cycle of internal toxicity.

And it all started with a feeling.

A recurring, unexamined, chemically reinforced feeling.

Now, most people are trained to think their mind is the boss of their life. That there's some fixed structure called "the mind" that floats around up there making decisions and planning goals. But one of my teachers once said, "There is no such thing as a mind. There is only frequency."

At first, that might sound strange. But the more you study how thoughts, emotions, and physiology interact, the more it becomes clear. What we call "mind" is really a current, a signal, a vibration, a frequency pattern that expresses itself through thoughts, words, and body states.

And once we understand frequency, we begin to understand God.

We begin to understand Life.

Here's where most people get tripped up: They believe that certain emotions are wrong. They judge their anger, suppress their grief, shame their jealousy. And in doing so, they don't just reject the emotion, they reject themselves.

They shut the door on their own power to co-create. They fall into victimhood, not because they are weak, but because they've been taught that only "positive" emotions are acceptable. And the moment we make any part of our emotional experience wrong, we hand its power over us.

That's when feelings become monsters. That's when we spiral. Because now, not only are we hurting, we also believe the pain is proof that we've failed. That we're broken. That we're unworthy of the life we desire.

But every emotion holds data. Inside anger is information about boundaries. Inside grief is the map of what mattered most. Inside fear is a signal for safety and presence. And inside every feeling is the raw material for transformation, if you're willing to sit with it.

When your emotional literacy grows, you begin to see how your thoughts, words, and feelings are producing reality in real-time, not years later. Not through complicated karmic webs, but right now. You become able to notice how the words you speak change your mood. How your posture changes your belief. How a shift in breath alters your ability to receive.

This is what I call the quickening.

At a certain point, your consciousness sharpens enough that you don't need to wait for hindsight to connect the dots. You begin to see, in the moment, how you are participating in your next outcome.

But to live like this, you get to recognize and transform the poison of judgment. Any trace of right or wrong clouds your vision. It traps you in a binary lens, through which you can't read the feedback your body is giving you.

Instead, you shift your perspective. You become a student of actions and results. You stop asking, "Was that good or bad?" and instead ask, "What did that produce?"

And here's the good news: Changing your emotional state doesn't have to be heavy or serious. In fact, sometimes the most profound shifts come from something ridiculous.

I once had a client who was stuck in a thought loop. Their body was tense, their mind was spinning, and no insight was breaking through. So, I asked them to stand on one foot, hop in a circle, and sing "Jingle Bells" as loud as they could.

They looked at me like I was insane.

But they did it anyway.

And within seconds, something cracked open. They started laughing. Their breath dropped. The inner noise quieted. Because that absurd act broke the spell of mental seriousness. It pulled them out of the program, out of the loop, and into presence.

The nervous system responds to movement. To sound. To rhythm. To surprise. So, when you shift your state, you move your chemistry. And when you shift your chemistry, you change your frequency. And when you change your frequency… you change your life.

This is the frequency of transformation.

It's not something you have to earn.

It's something you learn to feel.

And once you do, it becomes your compass.

Not the thought about how you want to feel.

The feeling itself.

Your emotions are not obstacles.

They are messengers.

They are teachers.

And when you stop trying to escape them, when you open the door and listen, they will guide you home.

The Fast Lane to Change: Skipping the "How"

A lot of clients come to me brimming with ideas. Brilliant ones. Heart-led, soul-aligned, potentially world-shifting. But then, just as that spark ignites, something starts to dim the light. The same pattern I've seen over and over again creeps in.

But how am I going to do it?

What are the first steps?

What if I fail?

The mind starts to negotiate against the soul. A thousand internal objections form a wall that stands between inspiration and execution. Suddenly, the excitement is gone, buried under a weight of logistics, timelines, doubt, and fear.

The longer someone stays stuck in the question of how, the more despondent they become. Their life force, once pulsing and alive with possibility, begins to shrink. Dreams that once danced at the edge of their awareness now feel far away, unreachable, even silly. And as their energy lowers, so does their belief in those dreams. They begin to settle. To tolerate. To fold themselves into the safe, familiar rhythms of a life they never really chose, just accepted.

Eventually, their days become spreadsheets of survival. They're not dreaming anymore; they're counting. Counting how much time is left. Counting money and calculating whether they'll run out of one before the other.

And here's the wild part: It's not just people struggling financially who fall into this trap. I've worked with millionaires who lie awake at night with the same fear. The same ache. The same mental loop. *How do I hold on? How do I make sure it doesn't all slip away?*

Because the trap of *how* is universal.

But what if there were another way?

What if there were a shortcut, an elegant, heart-led, frequency-aligned way to skip over the mind's obsession with strategy and control?

What if change didn't require knowing how, but simply shifting into now?

This fast lane exists. And I've seen it work over and over again.

It begins with two words.

Oh wow.

That's it.

Oh wow.

Say them out loud. Try it now. Say them with feeling. Say them as if something extraordinary just happened. As if someone handed you the best news of your life. As if you just received a blessing so perfectly timed, so profoundly generous, it brought tears to your eyes.

Repeat it.

Oh wow.

The magic in those two words isn't in the words themselves. It's in the frequency you attach to them. It's the feeling of reverence. Of awe. Of unfiltered gratitude. It's the chemical compound your body releases when it believes that something good, something sacred, has just happened.

The secret is to feel the joy of receiving before you know what you've received.

You don't need to fill in the details. In fact, the more you try to construct what you're reacting to mentally, the more you dilute the purity of the experience. The key is to surrender to the sensation of gratitude, without naming the thing you're grateful for.

Imagine it's five years from now, and you've just received the news. You're crying. Laughing. Shaking your head in disbelief. Not because of what it is, but because of how it feels.

Oh wow.

No grasping.

No fixing.

No how.

Just presence.

Let that feeling fill your body. Let it rise in your chest and pour out through your voice. Let it teach your nervous system what it means to be secure, to be chosen, to be trusted by life.

This is how you skip the spiral. This is how you bypass the loop. Instead of trying to figure out what to do, you start by tuning into how you love to feel, and then you feel it now.

You create an emotional imprint before the physical proof arrives. And by doing so, you signal to your body, to your field, to Life itself, that you're already available for the next level of joy, the subsequent unfolding of grace.

At first, this might feel strange. Some people resist it. They're so conditioned to earn their joy, to explain it, to justify it, that they forget how to receive simply.

Speaking through a feeling, without needing to justify it with logic, is a skill. But it's one that anyone can develop. Sometimes, working with a coach who embodies this in their own life can make all the difference. Because the energy is contagious. And when someone mirrors that emotional freedom to you, your system begins to remember its own capacity for joy.

The more you practice this, the more natural it becomes. Eventually, you'll start to experience the results of this practice in real time.

The byproducts?

Deep, unwavering trust in life.

A feeling of fulfillment that isn't tied to outcomes.

The emergence of healthy, effortless boundaries.

A life lived in alignment with your highest spiritual choices.

A calm nervous system.

A courageous heart.

A clear, intuitive mind.

And most importantly, the ability to walk through life seeing it as a gift, not a grind. You begin to value the journey itself more than the scoreboard of achievements. Your happiness is no longer dependent on what you produce, but on how you participate. You realize the destination was never the point.

The fast lane isn't about rushing.

It's about remembering.

Remembering that the frequency of transformation doesn't live in your plan.

It lives in your presence.

It begins with two words.

OH WOW.

Chapter 6: Shame, Guilt, Blame, and Hate: The Four Locks

Understanding the Glue Holding the Patterns in Place

One of the most essential components of QLT™, the part that most people never see at first glance, is understanding that patterns aren't held in place by the pattern itself. The pattern isn't the issue. It's not the habit, the trauma, the addiction, the behavior. Those are expressions. Symptoms. Echoes.

What holds the pattern in place is the glue.

And the glue is always emotional.

The four most powerful adhesives in the human system, shame, guilt, blame, and hate, are what bind people to the very cycles they are trying to escape. You can name your patterns. You can trace them. You can even temporarily interrupt them. But if the glue remains unaddressed, the pattern will find its way back, again and again and again.

The greater the intensity of these four emotional frequencies, the more deeply lodged the pattern becomes in someone's nervous system and identity. Shame whispers, "This is who I am." Guilt declares, "I should have known better." Blame says, "This is their fault." Hate screams, "Someone must be punished."

Together, these four forces create a self-imposed nightmare, a looping reality where beliefs harden, distort, and then manifest in physical, emotional, and relational suffering.

When someone enters the shame-blame-guilt-hate cycle, they are not simply experiencing intense emotions; they are undergoing a total hijacking of their chemistry. Their body begins producing more and more toxicity. Cortisol floods the system. Their immune function lowers. Their digestion weakens. Their sense of self shrinks. Their nervous system lives on high alert.

And as their internal world becomes more chaotic, their outer world reflects it.

Their life begins to produce evidence of that internal war: broken relationships, financial setbacks, chronic illness, isolation, stagnation, addiction. The fruit of the pattern continues to show up, not as punishment, but as a mirror. And as long as they remain attached to the glue, they will unconsciously re-create the pattern they are desperate to avoid.

Why?

Because the glue feels like truth.

It feels familiar. It feels earned. Shame masquerades as humility. Guilt feels like penance. Blame becomes a form of control. And hate becomes both a sword and a shield, a weapon to fend off anyone who dares to challenge the false self.

Using QLT™, we do not begin by attacking the pattern. We don't rush to fix behavior or reframe beliefs. We go to the glue first. Always.

Because, unless we address the emotional charge binding the pattern to the identity, the structure will rebuild itself in a new form.

Shame, when left unprocessed, is especially dangerous. It causes the individual to internalize everything that happens in their life, every mistake, every rejection, every perceived shortcoming, as proof of personal failure. They become the problem. Not the pattern. Not the trauma. Them.

When someone lives in this level of self-identification with shame and guilt, they begin to collapse inward. They isolate. They withdraw from relationships, responsibilities, even joy. They often fall into suicidal thinking, not because they want to die, but because they no longer believe they deserve to live.

The further they spiral, the more likely they are to seek relief through substances or compulsions. Alcohol. Pills. Porn. Gambling. Overworking. Undereating. Anything that offers a moment of silence from the self-hatred playing on loop.

And as they numb, they detach further from society's norms and values. They stop showing up for the things that once mattered. They retreat into subcultures that validate their worldview or enable their addiction. They start seeing the world through a lens of distortion, and the deeper the pain, the more the lens hardens.

Blame soon follows. Because blame feels safer than showing courage. It gives the illusion of power. So, they begin practicing it and perfecting it. They blame their boss, their ex, their childhood, the government, the system, the church. They build rehearsed monologues for every conversation, layering excuses and stories before anyone even asks a question.

And the more they blame, the more divorced they become from truth. The wider the schism between their story and reality, the more unstable they feel, mentally, emotionally, and eventually physically.

By the time hate enters, the pattern has become a fortress.

Hate becomes both a wall and a moat. It's how the person keeps others out. But more than that, it's how they protect the lies they've come to believe about themselves and the world. Hate is always loudest where the truth is closest.

So, when someone comes into their life with compassion, with a mirror, with truth, they attack.

They lash out.

They discredit, dismiss, and destroy anything that threatens the fragile house of mirrors they're living in.

This is not because they are bad. This is because they are terrified.

And the deeper someone is in this cycle, the more trapped they are in sympathetic nervous system dominance. They're no longer truly in their body. They are in defense. Their breath is shallow. Their vision narrows. Their heart races. Their jaw clenches. Their energy either explodes outward or freezes entirely.

In that state, you cannot reason with the mind.

Because they are not in their mind.

They are in survival.

They are having an out-of-body experience, even if they look calm on the outside. And this is where so many well-meaning coaches, therapists, or healers make a critical mistake: They try to do deep emotional work while the person is still disembodied.

That never works.

It can even cause more harm.

Before any transformation can occur, the practitioner empowers the person to return to their body. Reconnect to their breath. Reclaim security. Only then, once the glue has softened, can the pattern begin to release its hold.

Because once the glue is gone, the structure can't stand.

It was never the pattern that was powerful.

It was what held it in place.

How the Body Becomes Addicted to Emotional Chemicals

The process of addiction doesn't just begin with drugs, alcohol, or outside substances. It starts with chemistry. Whether the source of the substance is external, like cocaine, weed, or pharmaceuticals, or internal, like shame, guilt, and rage, the biological effect is strikingly similar. The body is always listening and constantly adapting and constantly imprinting the emotional and chemical patterns we repeatedly feed it.

Just like a person chasing their first high, returning again and again to that initial rush of euphoria, never quite reaching it, the body chases the chemistry of familiar emotions. If someone has lived their life in a state of self-hate, disappointment, or blame, their cells begin to prefer those states. Not because they are suitable for us, but because they are known. And what is known becomes safe. What is safe becomes home. Even if it's killing us.

Here's how it works.

Every emotion you feel releases a specific cocktail of chemicals into the bloodstream. That cocktail gets delivered to your cells. Each cell in your body has a receptor site, like a docking station, where those chemicals attach. Different chemicals fit into different receptor sites, just as a key fits into a lock. That's how the body receives and responds to the emotional signal.

But here's the wild part: The more a particular chemical floods the system, the more your cells begin to reproduce themselves with extra receptor sites for that chemical. If you live in chronic stress, your body will adapt by creating more docking stations for stress-related chemicals. If you live in self-loathing, you're growing cells that specialize in receiving the chemistry of self-loathing.

Over time, the cells of your body literally reshape themselves around your emotional baseline.

That means if your norm is anxiety, your body will develop a biological craving for anxious chemicals. If your go-to state is shame, your cells will expect shame. They'll call for it. And when they don't get it, you'll feel uneasy, like something is off. Not because something's wrong, but because your cells aren't getting the hit they've been conditioned to need.

This is how the body becomes addicted to its own emotional pain.

And this isn't just happening on an energetic level. It's happening chemically. Viscerally. Organically. The very fabric of your being is adjusting itself to match your emotional patterns.

And the cost is enormous.

When your cells build more receptor sites for shame, blame, or rage, they simultaneously build fewer receptor sites for health. For joy. For gratitude. For connection. The space those healthier signals would have taken up has been given to something else.

So, you can eat the right food, say your affirmations, go to therapy, do the breathwork, and still feel heavy. Still feel stuck. Still feel like your body is at war with your desire to grow.

Because on a cellular level, it is.

Your cells are not rejecting healing. They're just loyal to the chemistry they've been trained to expect. And that training happened one thought, one emotion, one pattern at a time.

Our bodies are constantly regenerating. Every second, we're making new cells. The lining of the gut turns over every few days. Skin renews every few weeks. The liver can regenerate itself almost entirely. And even the longest-living cells in the body, bone, brain, and heart, turn over entirely in seven years or less.

So, the question becomes: What emotional blueprint are your cells using to replicate themselves today?

Because whatever you're feeling most often, resentment, hope, fear, peace, is becoming part of your biology. And the longer your body lives in that frequency, the more it builds itself around it.

Now here's where it gets even more interesting.

Each chemical compound doesn't just affect your inner state; it also emits a frequency, a measurable vibration that gets broadcast into the field around you. That frequency becomes part of the signal you send to Life. And because reality is holographic, what you send out begins to reflect back to you.

So, your unprocessed shame doesn't just live in your chest.

It shows up in how people treat you.

In the job offers that pass you by.

In the partner that never fully commits.

In the tension in your neck, the fatigue in your body, the heaviness you can't shake.

And the more this reflection returns to you, the more you believe it.

"See? I knew I wasn't enough."

"I knew people would leave."

"This always happens to me."

And the moment you believe it, you feed it. You reinforce the belief. You produce more emotional chemicals. The cells get another dose. The receptors grow stronger.

This is how the glue forms.

This is how shame becomes identity.

How guilt becomes gravity.

How blame becomes worldview.

And how hate becomes armor.

Because when you're living in a biochemical loop of suffering, it begins to feel real. Tangible. Unquestionable. Not because it is the truth, but because your entire body has adapted to believe it.

And the more real it feels, the harder it becomes to let go. The more "proof" you see, the more your mind grabs hold. Until one day, the thought that you are your pain seems like fact.

But it isn't.

It's addiction.

Not in a moral sense.

In a biological one.

The same way someone can become addicted to a drug, a person can become addicted to despair. Not because they want to be in pain, but because their body is no longer calibrated to safety.

And so, the work isn't just mental.

It's chemical.

It's somatic.

It's cellular.

The QLT™ process doesn't just help someone "think better." It invites them to feel differently, so consistently, so profoundly, that their cells begin to change their allegiance, and their receptor sites start repopulating with room for joy. For safety. For ease.

Because healing isn't just about understanding your pain.

It's about upgrading your chemistry, so the pain no longer fits.

And when your body stops craving the emotions that hurt you...

You stop re-creating the life that mirrored them.

Dissolving the Locks: A Love-Based Response

If shame, guilt, blame, and hate are the locks that keep us imprisoned, then love is the only solvent that melts the bars and loosens the grip. Not the *idea* of love, not a poetic sentiment or affirmation in a mirror, but an actual experience of love: visceral, cellular, undeniable.

Once someone truly feels love, once it moves through their nervous system like warmth returning to frozen limbs, something miraculous begins to happen. The glue that held their pain in place starts to soften. The walls of their self-imposed prison don't collapse all at once, but they begin to crack. Light gets in. And more importantly, light gets out.

The lies that once felt so solid, like "I am broken," "I am unworthy," "I'll never be secure," start to lose their density. They begin to crumble, not because someone forced them away, but because the love now flowing through the system has rendered them obsolete. Like shadows at sunrise, they vanish not through effort, but by the presence of something greater.

This shift is more than emotional. It's energetic. It's neurological. It's chemical. And it's spiritual.

The body, which had once adapted to pain, starts to recalibrate toward peace. The cells, once loyal to the chemistry of suffering, begin to respond to something sweeter. And in that space, just beyond the collapse of the old story, a new vision begins to emerge.

At first, it's faint, a flicker, a soft imagining of what could be. But it grows. With each breath, with each moment of safety, the person begins to see a different version of themselves. Not the version shaped by trauma or survival, but the version that's always been quietly waiting beneath the debris. Whole. Capable. Creative. Worthy of joy.

As the feeling of love deepens, the individual no longer needs to reference their past in the same way. They don't have to tell their story to feel seen. They don't have to rehash their pain to feel real. And in one of the most unexpected turns, they realize something profoundly liberating:

There's nothing to forgive.

This is not denial. It's not bypassing. It's not saying that pain didn't happen or that injustice isn't real. But in the presence of divine love, forgiveness becomes irrelevant. Because forgiveness implies that something wrong was done that now requires pardoning. But love exists before right and wrong; it's transcendent. It says: There is nothing to correct, only something to remember.

From this higher frequency, the entire narrative begins to reorganize. The person sees not just what happened *to* them, but what happened within them. They realize the people who hurt them were also hurting. They see the patterns, the generational loops, the forgotten cries for help. And from this expanded view, compassion replaces resentment, not as a moral choice, but as a natural byproduct of clarity.

And when there is nothing left to fight, when the identity no longer depends on the story of being wronged, the body softens. The mind quiets. The soul returns to its seat.

This is the restoration of the divine blueprint.

This is when someone begins to remember who they really are.

Not a performer.

Not a fixer.

Not a survivor.

But a co-creator. A luminous being designed to live in partnership with life. To move with reverence. To speak with presence. To feel deeply and live freely and walk in a current of quiet joy.

From this place, things like boundaries are no longer a battle. They are a byproduct of self-respect. Discernment becomes intuitive. Decisions become graceful. There's no need to control or prove or protect, because the system is no longer braced against life.

It is open to it.

Alive in it.

Grateful for it.

This is not an escape from reality.

This is reality, when the glue is gone.

When love returns to the system, not as a concept, but as a felt sense of belonging, the locks fall off. Not because the person worked to free themselves, but because they finally stopped identifying with the prison.

And in that sacred exhale...

They begin to live.

Chapter 7: QLT™ Explained

What is QLT, really? A Toolset for Total Change

Let's go deeper.

The QLT isn't just a clever name. It's not a branding gimmick or another framework to memorize. It's exactly what it says it is: a direct shift in consciousness, a vertical jump to a higher frequency, a complete reorientation of how you experience reality, without having to process the past or "work through" the wound. QLT is a return to what's already true within you.

But to even begin this kind of shift, there's one foundational understanding required: The individual must make a choice to move from the operating system of right and wrong into the operating system of results and outcomes.

That sounds simple. But neurologically, emotionally, chemically, it's a complete transformation. The old paradigm of "right or wrong" lives in judgment; it's based in morality, fear, and the past. It keeps people locked in, proving, fixing, performing, or punishing. But outcomes are rooted in awareness. In creation. In clarity and choice. When we stop judging ourselves and others and instead ask, "What is the result I'm actually living? And what result do I want to live?", we reclaim authorship of our lives.

For the brain to make this leap, rewiring is required. And for that rewiring to stick, the individual has to feel the new truth in their body. Speech alone isn't enough. Empty words don't rewrite a nervous system. But when someone aligns their language with a felt sense, when their words are spoken from the inside out with resonance, something happens. Instantly. There is a shift in their field. A tangible change in frequency. Their body chemistry updates, and their perception of life updates with it.

In other words, they begin to see reality differently, sometimes at the very moment the new feeling is spoken.

To see something differently, the body must feel something differently. It's not mental. It's not logical. It's physiological. And the fastest way to generate a new feeling is to create new chemistry in the system.

Imagine someone addicted to cocaine. Their worldview is not neutral; it's filtered through the lens of craving, pain, and compulsion. Their reality is shaped by their chemistry. In the same way, someone stuck in a victim identity is living in a biochemical loop. Whether it's shame, fear, or resentment, the chemistry feeds the narrative, and the narrative feeds the chemistry. That's the loop that QLT breaks.

But the real magic begins when a person locates truth in their body. Not "their truth." Not opinion. Not story. But actual Divine truth. And truth has a feeling. You can't fake it. When someone speaks or imagines something profoundly true, their body knows. There's a relaxation. An openness. A click. Likewise, when someone states a lie, even if it's a lie they've believed for decades, the body contracts. There's discomfort, tension, or even nausea. QLT trains people to feel that difference and to orient their entire life toward what's true.

This alone changes everything.

Because our society is saturated in lies.

Industries have sold us falsehoods in every form: the fragrance industry, the corn industry, tobacco, alcohol, even some religions.

These lies have become so normalized that most people don't even recognize them as lies. They've gone numb. Disconnected. Desensitized to their own internal compass. And once that compass goes offline, people stop trusting themselves. They stop trusting others. They stop trusting life.

QLT turns the compass back on.

And when people begin to feel truth, objective, soul-anchored truth, they return to their own Divinity. They stop looking outside for permission. They stop outsourcing authority. They stop chasing healing and start becoming whole.

This transition from lies to truth doesn't just change how someone feels. It changes everything: relationships, finances, health, purpose. The shifts aren't incremental. They're exponential.

I remember working with a woman who hadn't spoken to her mother in over thirteen years. She'd been in therapy for two decades, trying to process the wounds caused by her mother. She'd been told countless times by professionals that she needed to forgive her mom. But she couldn't. She refused. The pain was too big. Too old. Too familiar.

When we sat down, I said something that caught her off guard.

"You don't have to forgive her."

She blinked, surprised. "What do you mean? Every therapist has told me I have to forgive her."

I smiled gently. "You don't. Not at all. Just tell me this… If nothing changes, if you stay on the current trajectory, what will your life feel like five years from now?"

She paused, then said honestly, "I'll still be bitter. Still resentful. Still stuck."

I nodded. "Beautiful. That's clear. Now let's play. Just pretend, for a moment, that something changed. Pretend you somehow forgave her. Not because she deserved it. Not because it was required. But just for fun. What's different in you five years from now?"

Her voice softened. Her eyes began to well up with tears. "I'd finally be free."

"Free from what?"

She swallowed. "Free to live my life."

"Say that again," I encouraged.

She did. And again. And again. And each time, something transformed. Her body let go. Her face shifted. She began to cry, not from sadness, but from the relief of finally letting go of something she'd carried for decades. Just by pretending. Not processing. Not forgiving. Just stepping into a new outcome long enough to feel it.

That moment changed her. But that wasn't the only miracle.

She was at a fasting retreat when we did our session. Later that night, she went back to her room and checked her phone. Her mother had called. For the first time in thirteen years. Left a voicemail. And said, "I just wanted to tell you… I love you."

They had not spoken in over a decade and neither had planned to. But when a shift occurs in one person's field, it ripples. We are all entangled in the quantum. And when someone leaps, everything attached to them feels the tug.

This is why QLT works even when the person you're healing with isn't in the room. Because in the quantum field, they are.

I've seen it again and again.

There was a couple whose daughter had severe allergies. They asked me if I could help treat her. I wondered when the allergies started.

"She's always had them," they said. "She was born with them."

That caught my attention. Allergies are often a sign of suppressed grief and fear. And if a baby is born into those frequencies, it means those energies were present during conception and gestation.

I asked more.

They told me they'd had nine miscarriages before she was born. And yet, they insisted their daughter was carried in peace. "The doctors said everything was fine," they said, almost defensively.

But their words were rushed. Their tone disconnected. They had never fully touched their grief.

I explained that their daughter's body might be expressing the very emotions they had never felt. So, I guided them into a visualization, inviting them to re-conceive and re-carry their daughter from a place of trust, gratitude, and reverence. As they did, something shifted in them. And as it did, the allergies in their daughter disappeared.

The body listens. The field responds.

This is the Quantum Leap.

It's not a theory. It's a lived shift in frequency that rewrites what you experience. When someone is stuck in resentment, fear, or bitterness, they live in one timeline, one lifeline of consequences and manifestations. But when that person leaps into appreciation or presence, they exit that loop and enter a new one. And the external world adjusts.

Even your taste buds can change.

There was a woman who loved wine. She had a favorite bottle she'd drink at home, a sensory comfort. But after experiencing a major breakthrough during a session, she went home and opened the wine… and it tasted off. She tried another bottle, same kind, different vintage. Still bad. She called me, confused.

"What's happening?" she asked.

I told her the truth.

"When your chemistry changes, your taste changes too. Your frequency no longer matches that behavior. That wine isn't for you anymore."

This is the deeper truth of addiction.

Instead of fighting the substance or declaring yourself powerless, QLT helps you shift your internal world so completely that the old behavior no longer belongs. It's not willpower. It's resonance.

That's why I don't teach people to say, "I am an alcoholic, and I am powerless." That cements identity into the past.

Instead, they say, "I am sober. I have reclaimed my power."

This is the essence of QLT.

We don't process wounds. We don't analyze why you're stuck. We don't rehearse the story.

We change your energy.

We leap timelines.

And in the new frequency, the old behaviors, identities, and pain simply don't exist.

They've been replaced… by something alive.

By something true.

By you.

The Difference: No Processing, Remembering the Future

The difference here is everything.

Most people get stuck in processing. It becomes a lifestyle. A full-time job. An identity. And many healing modalities, even the well-meaning ones, keep people circling endlessly in what we could call the "ing" phase: processing, integrating, hoping, improving, working through it. People will spend years here, good people, devoted people, feeling like they're moving forward simply because they're exhausted from all the inner work they're doing. But fatigue is not freedom. And just because something feels deep doesn't mean it's effective.

This is where QLT breaks away entirely. Those "ing" states rarely produce an actual shift in body chemistry. They might bring small insights, new perspectives, a few emotional releases, a fresh journal entry or two, but they don't rewrite the system. They don't create an energetic rupture in the pattern. Without that, the subconscious doesn't change. And if the subconscious doesn't change, the reality won't either.

You cannot "work through" your way into a new lifeline. You have to leap.

When a person experiences an actual energetic jump, a move from the sympathetic nervous system (fight, flight, freeze) into the parasympathetic (ease, safety, openness), a whole new field of awareness becomes available. The body lets go. The system unlocks. And just like that, the individual begins to see their life from this new state of being.

Not later. Not after ten sessions. Now.

In that state of ease, it's as if they're standing at the edge of a brand-new lifeline, one they've never walked before but already know. They begin to interview participants from this future self's reality.

Who do I become? What does it feel like to live there? What decisions do I make when peace, not fear, is in the driver's seat? These questions are no longer abstract. The answers don't come from theory or hope. They come from the body, now rewired in real time.

They come from the character they've just become.

This is what we mean when we say the difference is "no processing." We don't need to analyze the past to leave it. We get to embody the present as if the future has already arrived.

And here's where it gets even more powerful. One of the most critical inflection points in this process is what I call the "fluffle moment", the unexpected challenge, the old trigger, the thing that used to throw you off. The real question is: When that thing shows up in your new timeline, what do you do now?

This is where everything is revealed. The moment the person answers, from their new state of ease, they aren't just describing what they would do; they are programming it. They are instructing their subconscious with a new pattern. A conscious command, wired with emotion and spoken with embodiment.

And when that happens, the nervous system takes note.

Because if you have to think about the proper response in the moment, it's already too late. Thinking is too slow. You'll default to the past unless the future is rehearsed and installed. The only way to reliably respond from a higher level is to program it while you're already living in it, while your body is safe, your heart is open, and your mind is in coherence.

So, we don't process.

We rewire.

We rehearse.

We install.

We leap.

And when we do, we move into a new lifeline where the behavior, the response, the ease are automatic. Because it's who we are now. Not who we're trying to become. Not who we might be one day if we work hard enough.

But who we already are as soon as we stop trying to fix it and start living from the truth that we are already free.

How Outcome Focus Unlocks the Subconscious

When we talk about outcomes, we're not just talking about goals or results. We're not just speaking in terms of numbers, checklists, or achievements that can be measured and filed away. We're talking about something far more intimate than that. An outcome, in the way we use it here, is a first-person personal experience. It is not just what you desire to have; it's what you would love to live inside of.

That difference changes everything.

For example, a person might say, "I would love to have $200,000 in the bank." And sure, that's a goal, a tangible result. Something you can track and even celebrate. But what often happens when people hit that kind of target? There's a brief high, maybe a fleeting moment of satisfaction, followed almost immediately by the question, *What's next?* The goalpost moves. The emptiness returns. And the cycle of striving begins again.

In that loop, the manifestation process gets distorted. The individual starts to believe that either they didn't dream big enough or that the process itself is slow, complex, or unpredictable. I've seen it countless times. The person achieves something externally, but the internal wiring hasn't shifted. They hit the result, but they still feel like they're chasing something.

This is why we don't teach people to chase results. We teach them to create outcomes.

Because when you speak an outcome and feel it in your nervous system, you're not talking about what you hope to get *someday*. You're stepping into the reality of already living it. And that subtle shift? That's what the subconscious responds to. That's what changes the chemistry.

Let me make it more tangible.

Take the example of someone who longs to feel seen and validated by a parent. The result-oriented version of that might look like: *I want to prove myself by building a successful business.* That's still focused on the outer form. But an outcome sounds like this: *I finally heard my dad say, "I'm really proud of you, son. You've done an incredible job with your life."*

Now pause. Feel the difference.

Even just reading those words, you might notice your body respond. A lump in the throat. A softening in the chest. Maybe a tear forms, or your breath slows. That's the body starting to experience the outcome as real. That's a biochemical signature, not just a concept. And when the feeling becomes embodied, when the emotion lives in the present tense, the manifestation accelerates dramatically.

This is not abstract. It's physics.

The stronger the alignment between the words you speak, the vision you see, and the emotion you feel, the faster that reality forms around you. When we work in outcomes instead of results, things that would typically take years begin to happen with astonishing speed.

One client I worked with had just completed a three-year business plan with a coach. The strategy was solid. The projections were conservative, logical, and carefully laid out: double the business year over year, step by step, until they reached their target. Admirable. Smart. Linear.

We started working together around September, and I remember saying, "With what you're doing here, using this system, I believe your timeline is going to collapse. You're not waiting three years."

By May, just eight months later, they had hit their Year Three target in revenue.

And here's what's even more important: That client had been subconsciously building the business not just for freedom or income, but to prove something to their dad. To show they had value. That they would amount to something.

That's a familiar pattern.

Many people are unconsciously building their life to satisfy a wound instead of living from a healed outcome. So, we flipped it. Instead of continuing to manifest from the pain, we focused on the outcome. I asked, "What would it feel like to have the relationship with your dad already that you're trying to earn through success?"

We worked from that place.

They began to embody the feeling of already being seen and already being validated. Already being secure enough, loved. And what happened? The business soared. The conversations shifted. The energy freed up. The hustle softened. And reality rearranged to meet the new vibration.

Because when you stop trying to prove your worth and instead feel your worth, you stop pushing. You start creating.

This is why outcome-based work doesn't just make manifestation faster; it also makes it cleaner. You're not manifesting from lack or from trying to heal through external success. You're living from alignment, and alignment always brings acceleration.

So, ask yourself, sincerely and honestly:

What am I really trying to feel?

And what would change if I let myself feel that now, before anything external shifts?

That's where the leap lives.

Not in the strategy. Not in the steps.

But in the shift from thinking about your future… to feeling it.

Right here.

Right now.

Chapter 8: Transforming Your Painful Past

▍Stories From the Edge: What 20 Minutes Can Do

Over the years, I've heard the same sentence so many times, in different voices, from other faces, that I could almost mouth it before they say it:

"I got more out of 20 minutes with you than 20 years of therapy."

It's not a statement of ego. It's a reflection of what becomes possible when you speak the language of the body, the subconscious, and the truth, directly, without filter, without delay.

Let me show you.

We'll start with my own story.

I've shared before that I had a speech impediment as a child. The words used to get stuck in my throat, like my voice didn't trust itself to come out. As I got older, that shifted into a stutter, and with it came a deep, gut-wrenching fear of speaking in front of groups. My body would tighten, my breath would vanish, and my nervous system would revolt. The panic wasn't logical; it was cellular.

And then, one day, that all changed.

In less than ten minutes, something shifted in me. And I don't mean a slow fade. I mean a rupture, a reroute. I went from locked up to flowing, from hesitant to clear. It was as if the internal story that had gripped my throat for years finally exhaled. That moment wasn't just about words. It was about reclaiming my voice. About stepping back into the authority I'd unknowingly handed over to fear. And once it moved, it moved fast.

But the shift didn't stop there.

My instructor looked at me and asked something like, "So now that you speak clearly, what's new and different for you in five years?"

At first, my thoughts were racing. I didn't know what I was going to do next week, so I had no idea what five years would look like. My mind scrambled for an answer, grasping at nothing.

The instructor pressed. And then something came out of my mouth with no thinking, no planning, no logic: "I am leading my own classes."

The words surprised me. The first time they came out, no feeling was attached, only surprise. I heard myself say it and thought, *where did that come from?*

The instructor pressed again. "Say it again."

So, I did. "I am leading my own classes."

And something began to happen.

Every time I said it, my body began to heat up. My voice grew stronger with every repetition. Something was aligning, words and feelings fusing into one current. I began to experience the power of an instantaneous alignment, and I started to see my new life. Not as a distant hope. Not as a visualization exercise. Not as wanting, hoping, or planning.

I was experiencing a vivid memory of my future as if it had already happened.

Once I could see it, I had the confidence, the clarity, and the commitment to transform my old life into my new one. The path was no longer abstract. It was real. It was mine.

I never would have believed that a person who was terrified to speak in public, who stuttered and sweated just to get through three minutes in front of a group, would be doing what I am doing now. But that's exactly what happened. And as this transformation occurred for me, it does so for all of our clients. As this shift takes hold, their levels of loving life and themselves begins to grow exponentially.

That's the thing about truth: It doesn't require time. It requires access.

I've seen the same principle unfold in countless others.

There was a man I worked with who was experiencing tremors from Parkinson's. His hands shook. His body was betraying him in ways he couldn't control. When we met, he looked worn down, not just from the condition but from the fight. He had been trying everything, but it wasn't working. We spent about twenty minutes together, working through the system using QLT™. And by the end of that short session, 60 to 70 percent of his symptoms were gone. Just… gone. And the change didn't fade; it continued to improve after that.

Then there was a woman in one of my classes. We were mid-session, deep in a particular exercise, when I noticed that she was squinting. Her brow furrowed. Her head tilted, like she was trying to bring the room into focus.

"Everything okay with your eyes?" I asked.

"It just got really blurry," she said, confused. "All of a sudden, I can't see clearly."

"Are you wearing contacts?"

"Yes."

"Can you take them out?"

She hesitated, unsure. But she removed them.

And then, her whole face shifted.

"Oh my gosh," she exclaimed, blinking. "I can see clearly… without them. If I put them back in, everything's blurry."

Her prescription, her reality, had just flipped in real time. The body had recalibrated to a new state, and her eyes followed suit.

But perhaps one of the most profound stories I've witnessed involved a man who had been homeless, battling fear and abandonment for two decades. He'd been in therapy for twenty years, trying to untangle the wound, twenty years of effort. And still, the pain persisted.

When we sat down, I asked gently, "What if the reason you're not getting results… is that what you're working on is a lie?"

He blinked at me, startled. "A lie?"

"Yes," I said. "Because when you work on a lie, you stay trapped in it. But when you find the truth, freedom is fast."

So, I asked, "What's your real fear?"

He looked down. "I don't know."

I leaned in. "Say instead, 'I choose to know.'"

He rolled his eyes. Got irritated. "Like that's gonna do anything."

"Just say it."

So, he did. But not gently. Not peacefully. He said it with tension, with disbelief, with anger. "I choose to know," like he was daring me to prove him wrong. Again. And again. Ten… twelve… fifteen times.

And then, something happened.

His tone changed. His eyes softened. And with full breath and body, he said, "I choose to know… as a fact."

Immediately, I asked again, "What's your fear?"

This time, there was no pause.

"Love," he said.

The room froze.

His voice had just spoken the truth his body had known all along.

Tears filled his eyes. Mine too. Others in the room began to cry. Not out of sympathy, but recognition. Because we all knew that we had just witnessed a man speak truth for the first time in twenty years.

And from that moment forward, his life changed. He entered into a relationship. Became a successful author. Not writing theory, but sharing the raw, honest truth of what it meant to fear love so deeply… and then finally let it in.

Another time, I was teaching a free group class. Doctors and patients filled the room. Many of the physicians had been struggling to help their patients get results. One woman was there, her body burdened with a list of symptoms: seizures, high blood pressure, chronic pain. She was on muscle relaxers, painkillers, and anti-seizure meds, and had been for years. Still, nothing was truly working.

I wasn't treating her. I was just giving a talk on language, emotions, and the nervous system. A simple intro. But she raised her hand.

"I get how stress affects the immune system," she said. "But what about chronic pain?"

"Just talk," I said.

And she did.

Within thirty seconds, she started saying the exact phrase over and over: "I don't feel…"

"I don't feel angry. I don't feel hate. I don't feel frustrated."

The pattern was loud.

I said gently, "Say, 'I give myself permission to feel again.'"

She repeated it, fast, mechanical. Again. And again. The third or fourth time, something cracked open in her system.

She had a seizure.

People in the room began to panic. Doctors started to rise from their seats. But something inside me kicked in.

"Sit down," I said. Calm, clear. "I've got this."

Even as my own thoughts whispered doubts, something deeper took over.

"No sympathy," I told the room. "If you're going to feel sorry for her, step outside. She doesn't need your pity. She needs permission."

I worked with her, breath by breath, statement by statement. "I choose to make this okay," I told her. She repeated it. Slowly, the seizure subsided. Her system began to stabilize.

By the end of the class, she was still there, calm, present. I asked her to stay, and we talked again afterward.

That's when I learned the rest of her story.

Her husband, her first husband, had woken her up one morning at 4 a.m., handed her a note, and then walked outside and shot himself. A shotgun and a rifle at the same time. That kind of trauma doesn't just leave scars; it carves silence into the body. She had never processed it. Had never truly felt what it did to her. She focused on how it affected her kids. But her own grief was buried. Frozen.

She'd told me that one of her deepest dreams was to dance with her new husband, just one more time before she died. She was in her early 70s. Frail. Slouched. Ashen-skinned. When she first arrived, she could barely walk without leaning on him for support.

But something began to shift.

She signed up for five sessions.

Before we'd even begun the first one, she had already taken herself off her pain meds and reduced her muscle relaxers by over 75%. She was dancing around the living room. The seizures stopped. Her husband, who hadn't been able to leave her alone for more than a few minutes in six years, finally could.

Between sessions four and five, I was scheduled to teach another group of doctors. She was supposed to attend and share her story.

But she didn't come.

She was on a cruise with her husband.

The first cruise she'd been on in years. And this time, she could walk. Not just to board the ship, but move freely. She danced. She laughed. She participated in everything. And the next time I saw her; she told me she'd been taken off all her blood pressure meds. Off seizure meds. Off muscle relaxers. And one day, she looked at me and said, a little sheepishly:

"I'm a little disappointed today."

"Why?" I asked.

"Well," she said, "I went dancing last night… but I could only dance every other song."

From not being able to stand… to dancing every other song? In a month?

That's not healing. That's resurrection.

And all of that, every shift, every breakthrough, began in the first 20 minutes.

Healing From Presence and Possibility

Most traditional modalities start by walking backward. They assume that in order to move forward, we must dissect the past, again and again. The wound is reopened, the story retold, the memory made sharp. But with the QLT, we don't walk backward; we don't need to. What sets this work apart is that it doesn't require a person to fix the past in order to be free from it. There is no need to solve every piece of your personal history. You don't have to map the maze of your childhood in order to exit it. Freedom isn't waiting at the end of a long road of emotional excavation. It's right here, hidden in the now, ready to rise the moment you're willing to let a new future speak louder than your past.

The way we approach transformation is simple, yet radical. Instead of digging for old pain, we point to new possibility. We let the vision of what's next become so vivid, so embodied, so energetically real, that the pain of the past begins to dissolve, not through effort, but through contrast. When your system is filled with the resonance of what's coming, the ache of what has been no longer holds the same gravitational pull, the frequency changes. The story shifts. The emotional glue that held those old scenes together loses its stickiness.

It's not that the past didn't happen. It's that it no longer gets to narrate your future.

In fact, one of the most overlooked dynamics in the healing space is this: The more you speak something, the more powerful it becomes. Not because the event itself is growing, but because your identity is being shaped by your retelling. When someone revisits the same traumatic story over and over, adding color, emotion, meaning, and detail, it doesn't just remain a memory; it becomes a lens. And with every repetition, that lens gets thicker, more distorted, more attached to the storyteller's sense of self. Even the embellishments become truth. Even the parts we fabricated to feel seen become fixed in the subconscious. And soon, we are not just recalling our past. We are reinforcing it.

That's why our methodology spends very little time inside the content of what happened. We're not interested in building a more elaborate story about your pain. We're interested in making space for a new one.

But there's a nuance here, a sacred step many systems miss. We don't bypass the body. In fact, before we touch a single emotion, we bring the person back into their body. This is the key. Most modalities try to help people process feelings while they're still disassociated, floating, disconnected from sensation. But you can't heal what you won't feel. And you can't feel what you aren't willing to inhabit.

So we begin with embodiment, gentle, grounded reconnection. We guide the person inward, not into the mind, but into the breath, the gut, the pulse, the present. We ask: "What's happening in your body, right now?" And we wait. We let the body speak before the story. As this reconnection deepens, the nervous system starts to soften. Not just the adult self, but the younger one too, the part that lived the trauma, felt the terror, didn't have the tools. That version of you begins to feel something it may never have felt before: safety.

When the body begins to feel secure, everything changes.

From this place, the individual can revisit an old emotional imprint, not from the fragmented ego, but from the anchored presence of divine love. They don't have to relive the trauma. They only have to be with it. And that simple presence, that steady witness, opens the door to something profound: reversal.

Reversal isn't about pretending the past didn't happen. It's about experiencing it from a different seat in consciousness. It's the moment your body no longer flinches. The moment your heart remains open. The moment the memory arises and no longer hijacks your breath.

And in that moment, something unexplainable happens: The pain doesn't need to be fixed. It simply no longer rules.

As the reversal unfolds, a person's inner vision clears. They begin to see a future they couldn't access before, not because it wasn't available, but because they were still bonded to the frequency of their former self. The leap begins. A new storyline takes shape. Not forced, not scripted, but revealed.

Because the truth is this: You can't heal what you can't be with. And you can't be with something if your system is still at war with it.

So, we slow down. We get in the body. We let the present become real. And we allow love, not logic, not reprocessing, to meet the pain.

That's where the leap begins.

Not from analyzing what broke you.

But from remembering what you've always been: a genius of divine design, whole and capable beyond measure.

The Myth of the Long Healing Journey

When someone says they're on a healing journey, there's usually an unspoken agreement underneath. The agreement says: Something is broken, and it must be fixed. Something happened, and now I must spend my life trying to undo it. And so, the journey begins, framed by the assumption that there's always a trauma to heal from, always a wound to trace back to, always something lurking in the past that needs to be resolved before the future can be lived.

But what if that assumption isn't valid?

What if healing isn't the foundation of the path, but a byproduct of something greater?

What we're doing here is not about healing in the traditional sense. It's not about endlessly circling the drain of childhood, collecting reasons for why things are hard. It's not about staying in the loop of fixing and re-fixing your inner self. The journey we're on is a journey of continual upgrades, a forward-facing, future-rooted unfolding of possibility. And yes, healing may occur. Deep healing. But it doesn't come because we chased it. It comes because we stopped pursuing the pain and started listening to what was calling us forward.

That shift alone changes everything.

Because when your orientation is toward what's returning, toward what's being restored, reawakened, and revealed in you, your energy moves forward. Your spirit lifts. You begin to live with a quiet readiness, a holy anticipation. Life no longer feels like something you're dragging behind you. It becomes something you're meeting, moment by moment, with outstretched hands.

Other modalities often focus on what needs to be released, let go of, or banished. They invite the client to pour attention into the unwanted, to dissect, process, name, and ultimately try to eject the parts of themselves that carry pain. But here's the paradox: When your attention is fixated on what you want to get rid of, you're still in relationship with it. You're still feeding it. You're still making it real.

What we've found is that true freedom doesn't come by trying to get rid of anything. It comes when you stop fighting altogether and turn your attention toward what's returning. You stop trying to erase, and you start making room to receive.

And that subtle reorientation creates a profound shift. Because instead of slogging through your inner shadows, trying to earn your way into light, you begin to experience life as a river, carrying you into greater and greater expressions of love, trust, and embodied peace. Life becomes less about what you've survived, and more about what you're now capable of stewarding.

There's an entirely different texture to that kind of journey. Not one of urgency or pressure, but of reverence.

This path does become a practice, but not the kind of practice that's rooted in hyper-vigilance or self-correction. It's not a daily audit of what still needs fixing. It's a continual coming home to the experience of peace. It's a devotion to curiosity, to the feeling of alignment, to the ever-expanding capacity to live with wholeness. It's learning how to meet each moment from a deeper place of rest.

And in that way, the path becomes sacred.

Not because it's hard.

But because it's true.

You begin to trust not just life, but yourself, your own rhythm, your own timing, your own unfolding. You start to move from obligation into invitation. From effort into attunement. From chasing relief to receiving joy.

So yes, the work we do here can absolutely become a lifelong path. But it's not a life spent trying to avoid pain; it's a life lived in increasing degrees of inner peace. Increasing softness. Increasing sovereignty. Increasing reverence for the mystery of it all.

It's the difference between trying to heal a wound and finally learning how to live.

Chapter 9: Healing Through Love

The Power of a Profound Love Experience

Some of the most powerful healing tools I've ever witnessed from the QLT™, techniques that bypassed decades of traditional therapy, emerged from my work with survivors of the most unspeakable traumas. I didn't discover them in textbooks or certifications. They were revealed in the sacred space of presence, through trial and trembling grace, in sessions with individuals who had suffered under the darkest corners of human cruelty: survivors of satanic ritual abuse and MK Ultra.

These weren't clients looking for surface-level mindset shifts. These were women and men who had endured horrors most people couldn't stomach hearing about, let alone survive. Many had been in therapy for fifteen, sometimes twenty years, chasing fragments of relief. And yet, despite the endless hours of analysis, talk, and medication, the core trauma still pulsed beneath the surface. They were still triggered, still locked out of their own bodies, still struggling deeply with intimacy. Especially sexual intimacy.

Some of the women I worked with had been gang-raped on LSD at the age of six. Six years old! Drugged. Violated. Fragmented. Their earliest encounters with the body were not of innocence, but of terror and betrayal. So, when people ask why someone "can't just move on," I desire to look them in the eye and say, "Can you imagine what that child felt as she lay there, hallucinating, unable to scream for help?" It doesn't just leave scars. It rewrites the body's relationship with safety, with trust, with self.

Nevertheless, I would love to share what happened next because while these traumas are authentic, heavy, and deeply rooted, so is the power of love. Not the soft, poetic love we quote on greeting cards. I'm talking about the unshakable, unwavering force of love that can rearrange chemistry, rewrite nervous systems, and resurrect a soul that long ago abandoned hope.

Here's how the exercise begins.

We return to that moment. Not to relive it, not to process it again, but to do something entirely different. We go back, not to the horror itself, but to the little girl who endured it. In the imagination, we find her. She's there, somewhere, frozen in time. Lying on the floor. Forgotten by everyone except her own nervous system. And then, in the mind's eye, we go to her. We pick her up. Gently. Tenderly. Without a word, we carry her to a place that feels safe. Somewhere quiet. Somewhere clean. Somewhere that doesn't smell like terror.

And then, we do nothing. We just hold her.

We hold her, not with words, not with analysis, not with sympathy, but with presence. With love. With the simple, steady warmth of being there.

And I ask the adult, "What's happening in her body as you hold her?" This is not a metaphorical question. This is everything. What's her breathing like? Is her body tense or beginning to soften? Is she crying? If so, are they tears of panic or something else?

And as the adult begins to describe what's happening with the little girl, something extraordinary occurs. She begins to feel it in her own body. Her chest tightens when the girl's does; the fists unclench when hers do, the breath deepens in sync with hers. It's like time collapses, and the adult is no longer outside of the girl, watching from a distance; she is with her, in her. And for the first time, the little girl is not alone.

This is the pivot, the sacred turning point. The adult who has spent years dissociated from her own body, numb, frozen, guarded, starts to come back online. Not through cognitive reframing, but through embodied resonance. As she notices the girl's shoulders begin to drop, she realizes her own are doing the same. When she whispers, "She's still crying, but the tears feel different now," I often ask, "What's the difference?" And the answer usually comes softly: "They're not tears of terror anymore. They feel… like relief."

This is not imagination. This is biology. The body is registering safety for the first time in decades. The nervous system is recalibrating. The pattern is dissolving, not through force, but through love.

And then I ask the question that brings the unconscious into the light: "What did you do to make this possible?"

And always, after a pause, the same truth rises. "I just held her," she says. "I held her with love."

That's the moment. That's the medicine.

When the adult recognizes that the thing that softened her pain, that cracked open the door to trust, wasn't a brilliant technique or a years'-long plan, it was love, something profound settles in. She sees it clearly now: It wasn't about fixing her or saying the perfect thing. It was about being fully present, without judgment, in a state of unconditional love. That's what healed her. And in healing the girl, the adult began to heal too.

Now, here's something critical for anyone guiding this kind of work to understand: This process only works if the practitioner is operating from a particular level of consciousness. If you bring sympathy into the space, if you feel sorry for the client, if you hold judgment about the trauma, if you subtly carry the energy of "you poor thing," you will make things worse. Sympathy fractures. It separates. It positions the helper as superior and the wounded as broken.

For this work to unfold safely and effectively, the facilitator is required to empty themselves of all stories of right and wrong. They become a field of nonjudgmental presence. Neutral. Steady. Anchored in truth, not drama. If that container is clean, if it is rooted in love without distortion, the transformation can unfold rapidly, sometimes in less than twenty minutes.

That's the power of a profound love experience. It is not sentimental; it is surgical. It reaches into the very places therapy couldn't touch, because it speaks in the language the body remembers: presence. Stillness. Trust. Connection.

Love doesn't fix the past. It makes it irrelevant.

And when the child within finally feels secure, finally feels seen, finally feels held without needing to perform or justify her pain, she returns. And when she returns, so does the adult. Not the traumatized adult who has been performing healing for decades. But the one who is whole. The one who is here.

The one who finally knows what love feels like and who now knows she can offer it to herself.

Healing Through Remembering Our Divine Unity

Healing doesn't begin with medicine. It starts with memory, not memory of the past, but of truth. The kind of deep remembering that calls us back into the heart of who we really are. And over the past thirty-five years, both in my own spiritual practice and in the sacred work of coaching others, I've come to understand this: Most pain, disease, and suffering doesn't come from what happened to us; it comes from one simple, devastating misunderstanding.

The belief that we are separate from God.

This single illusion is the root of it all. Separation. Disconnection. The thought, "I'm alone. I've been left behind. I'm not enough. I must earn my place." It doesn't matter the language; we've all had our version of it. And every time someone believes they are separate from the Source of Love itself, an immediate and measurable shift takes place in the body. Stress floods the emotional system like a silent siren. Muscles tighten. The chest closes. The breath shortens. Judgment arises. First toward life. Then toward God. And finally, toward the self.

They begin to make life wrong.

They begin to make God wrong.

They begin to make themselves wrong.

And then they wonder why everything feels so wrong.

But it's not life that's broken. It's not the body, or the past, or the people around them. It's the belief, a belief that subtly shapes every thought, every feeling, every interpretation of experience. Most of the people I've worked with, beautiful, strong, open-hearted people, have been walking through life with a false narrative about how reality works. And the story often goes like this: "I have to be good enough to earn love. I have to prove I'm worthy of healing. I have to do something extraordinary to reconnect with God."

That story, beneath all its well-worn grooves, is built on a lie.

The truth is, we are already connected. Always have been. Always will be. We are children of God, not by achievement, but by nature. We don't need to become something more in order to be worthy of that connection; we just need to remember that we were never disconnected in the first place. It's not a journey of reconnection; it's a journey of recognition.

It is impossible to be separate from God. But it is entirely possible to believe that we are. And when we think it, we suffer. Not as punishment, but as a signal. A message from the body, the soul, the field, whispering, *you've forgotten the truth again.*

This is what I mean when I say that hell is not a place. It is a state of non-ease. A self-imposed exile. The more disconnected we believe we are, the more discomfort we feel. The body begins to break down under the weight of the illusion. Symptoms emerge, not as enemies, but as messengers. They are not here to be feared. They are here to be listened to. To guide us back.

Every illness is the body's asking for love.

Every diagnosis is a doorway.

Every flare-up is a flare, trying to lead us home.

When someone has a real experience with love, not just a memory of being cared for, but an embodied remembrance of *being* love, everything changes. They begin to return to their body. And as they come home to themselves, a new kind of ease begins to unfold. Not just emotional, but biological. Physiological. Cellular.

This ease is not metaphorical. It's measurable.

Just as a wound on the skin will begin to heal when properly cleaned, cared for, and placed in a safe environment, the body's internal wounds respond the same way. If you cut your hand, and you keep it clean, wrap it gently, and avoid contaminating it with more pain, your body will know what to do. Even if it's a deep cut. Even if it takes time. The body is wired for healing, and your inner genius knows exactly how to restore itself. It's only when we keep aggravating the wound, physically, mentally, emotionally, that it festers.

The same principle applies to chronic illness, emotional dysregulation, or spiritual dis-ease. When given the right internal conditions, the body repairs itself. But most of us have been taught to manage symptoms instead of listening to them. We try to numb or control the very signals that are trying to bring us back into harmony.

So what prevents healing? What poisons the system?

Toxicity. Not just the chemical kind, but emotional toxicity: anger, resentment, jealousy, hate, shame, guilt, blame. These emotional states don't just create discomfort. They create chemistry. They alter the very frequency of the body. They flood the system with stress hormones, suppress immune function, inflame tissues, and over time, give rise to what we call "disease." But these aren't random afflictions. They're the body's language, trying to show us where we've disconnected from love.

In our work, we don't call them symptoms.

We call them signals.

Signals that something is off. Something is misaligned. Something has been made wrong, life, the body, the self, and the body is simply responding to that distortion. It's not betraying you; it's trying to wake you up.

Healing is the natural byproduct of returning to truth.

Returning to ease.

Returning to unity.

And unity begins the moment we stop judging, when we stop dividing life into good and bad, right and wrong, deserving and undeserving. The moment we stop believing the lie of separation, the nervous system shifts. Breath returns. Peace returns. And the body, finally, can do what it was always designed to do.

Love isn't just a warm feeling. It is medicine, the most potent, precise, bio-intelligent frequency in existence. And when someone remembers that they are loved, without needing to earn it, fix themselves, or change anything about their being, their entire system relaxes into truth. That's what allows for restoration. Not force. Not effort. Not years of processing. Just truth.

And truth always brings us back to one thing:

You were never broken.

You only ever believed that you were.

And the moment you stop believing that lie, you begin to come alive.

Healing Through Love, Faith, and Action

Even in Scripture, when Christ healed someone, He rarely took credit for the healing Himself. Again and again, He pointed to something deeper, something already alive within the person.

"Your faith has made you well."

Not His power. Not their perfection. Not a list of spiritual accomplishments or religious rituals.

Their faith.

And not just any faith. Not the intellectual kind that recites verses and hopes for the best. But the kind that moves. That lives. That takes form as action. Scripture doesn't stop at "Have faith." It tells us plainly: "Faith without works is dead." Which also means, faith with action is life.

This is where most traditional therapy falls short. It tries to heal people through intellect, through insight, through memory. But healing doesn't come just from remembering the past; it comes from recognizing truth and then living from that place. And the most profound truth, the one that rewires every cell, reorganizes every belief, and restores the nervous system to peace, is love.

Not an idea of love. Not a theory. Not a "spiritual belief" or mantra repeated a hundred times.

An experience.

What heals people, consistently, across every session I've ever done, whether it's emotional trauma, chronic illness, or long-held patterns, is one thing, every time:

Love.

And not lowercase love. Not sentimental, surface-level love. Not conditional, co-dependent, self-sacrificing love.

I'm talking about Love with a capital L. The frequency of God. The organizing intelligence of the universe. The original language of the soul.

And for it to work as medicine, it requires a person to experience it directly.

A visceral experience to move them

To change and transform something in their body.

When someone has a genuine encounter with Love, you can feel it in the room. Their whole posture shifts. Their breath deepens. Their voice softens. The eyes begin to widen, not from fear, but wonder. They begin to see a new life. Not imagine it, see it. It's like a door opens and light floods in where there was only survival before.

And in that moment, the body starts to remember ease.

The field begins to re-pattern.

The chemistry changes.

Healing becomes not only possible, but inevitable. Because now they've touched the blueprint. They've remembered what's real.

But this is the part therapy often misses.

Having a breakthrough in a session means very little if it's not followed by action. Love can open the door, yes. But it's faith in that love that walks you through it. And that faith requires transforming into something embodied in choices, in steps, in bold moves that say, "I trust what I saw. I trust what I felt. I will live like it's true."

And this is where healing either accelerates or stalls.

If a person has a profound experience with Love but doesn't respond to it, doesn't take even one action that reflects this new reality, the nervous system begins to question the experience. The body needs confirmation that what it felt wasn't just a fluke, that this new state is secure to live in. And the only way it gets that confirmation is through behavior.

Every time someone takes a step toward their healed self, toward the version of them that already exists beyond the pattern, the healing deepens. The signal strengthens. The body calibrates to a new baseline. It no longer needs to protect the past, because it has proof that something truer is now being chosen.

And the more someone lives as if healing has already occurred, the faster it unfolds.

That's why I always say healing doesn't come through talking about love. It comes through being held by it and feeling it and choosing it and trusting it.

When someone allows Love to saturate their nervous system and then takes aligned action from that place, they don't need years of processing. They need presence. They need courage. They need to walk as if the miracle already happened, and watch as their life reshapes around the truth, they've finally allowed to enter their body.

Love is the medicine.

Faith is the activator.

Action is the agreement.

And when all three are in place, the healing isn't slow.

It's spontaneous.

Because the body always responds to truth.

Especially the truth that it was never broken, only waiting to be loved back into itself.

Chapter 10: Instant Results in Real Life

The Parkinson's Case: Healing Through Frequency

I met him during a Body Electronics workshop, a quiet man in his early seventies whose body betrayed a storm it could no longer contain. His right hand trembled constantly, a relentless rhythm that kept him awake most nights, the kind of tremor that doesn't just interrupt sleep, but sanity. His cognition was beginning to slip, too: moments of forgetfulness, disorientation, confusion creeping in like fog. It was Parkinson's, diagnosed years earlier. Worsening slowly, then all at once.

Before we even began the formal system work, I noticed something in his energy, a kind of unresolved tension. Not just in his body, but in his field. A story, unfinished, unspoken, was pressing against the surface of his skin. I had worked with enough clients by then to know that disease is never just physical. Especially not something like this. And so, I sat with him and asked if he was willing to explore the emotional component before we moved into the protocol.

He said yes. And something in his voice told me that even though he had been suffering for years, this was the first time anyone had asked that question.

We dropped in. He closed his eyes. And we went back, back through the years, back through the layers of identity, of memory, of story, until we arrived at a moment that seemed, on the surface, insignificant. He was five years old. A little boy. And he had just gotten into a heated argument with his father.

But this wasn't just any argument. This was the first time he remembered feeling insecure in his own body. His nervous system had gone into full-blown fight or flight, and it had never quite come back. The exchange with his father had locked in a core conflict about right and wrong. He couldn't articulate it as a child, but the emotional intensity of that moment had written something into his system. Something absolute. Something condemning.

He had carried that conversation in his cells for nearly seven decades.

As we worked, I asked him to describe what was happening in his five-year-old body. Not from the head, but from presence. From truth. He began to feel the heat of that childhood moment again, the pressure in his chest, the clench in his fists, the panic in his breathing. And then, as we dug a little deeper, we discovered the exact phrases he had spoken at that moment as a child. Words that had etched themselves into his psyche like a vow. Words spoken in fear, in rage, in separation.

And that was the turning point.

Because words hold frequency. And those words had not just shaped his thoughts; they had also shaped his biology. They had become a kind of internal decree, echoing through his life, influencing everything from his posture to his health to his sense of worth. This was the origin of the pattern. Not the diagnosis. Not the tremors. But this, this moment of misalignment, buried beneath a lifetime of logic.

So, I asked him to speak the reversal.

To find new words, aligned with truth, with love, with unity, and speak them into his body. At first, his voice shook. Emotion caught in his throat. But as the new phrases began to take root, something remarkable happened.

Right there, in the middle of a class of more than twenty people, his right hand began to stabilize.

The tremor, which had dominated his life for years, started to quiet. We all saw it. One by one, people in the room looked over, their eyes widening as they realized what was happening. This wasn't imagination. This was happening in real time. Before their eyes.

He kept speaking. Kept releasing. Kept choosing love over fear. And within fifteen to twenty minutes of focused reversal work, about sixty to seventy percent of the tremor had subsided. We didn't use a tool. We didn't use a drug. We used presence, memory, language, and love. And the body responded the way all bodies do when they are finally heard.

His healing didn't stop there. From that point forward, the improvements continued. Just began in that room had initiated a new trajectory for his health. The most beautiful part? It wasn't just the symptoms that improved. It was him. His spirit, his vitality, his youthfulness. It was as if someone had turned the light back on.

That's what happens when someone fully reverses the old decree. When they find the words that locked them in pain and speak new ones from a place of authority and love, something profound begins to take place at a cellular level. The memory embedded in the body starts to rewrite itself. Not just mentally, but physically, emotionally, spiritually. The shift is fundamental. It's measurable. It's visible.

This is the true healing path, not just eliminating symptoms, but rejuvenating the entire system. And I've seen it over and over again.

As a person begins to anchor in the frequency of truth and love, the body doesn't just return to baseline; it upgrades. They regain energy. They laugh more. They move with ease. Often, they begin to feel like they've gotten ten, fifteen, even twenty years of their life back. I've watched people improve their flexibility, endurance, even their sexual function, not through external treatment, but through internal coherence.

Because when the body feels secure again, when the story running inside the system has shifted from fear to love, it stops fighting. It stops protecting the wound. And instead, it starts to play again. To explore. To create. To feel.

The same body that trembled in terror now reaches for life.

The same man who couldn't sleep now walks without fear.

Not because he escaped his past, but because he rewrote its meaning.

That is the power of frequency.

That is the power of presence.

That is the power of love made tangible, spoken aloud, and acted upon.

Autism, Pain, and Posture: When the Body Feels Safe

She walked into the room on the first day of class with her head low and her shoulders curled forward, like her entire body had been taught to shrink away from the world. She was sixteen, quiet, and deeply sensitive. I could feel it before she even spoke; her nervous system was in high alert, her eyes scanning but rarely locking, her voice almost imperceptible. When she did make eye contact, it was fleeting, like a door cracked open just long enough to see there was light behind it, then closed again out of habit, out of protection.

She had autism, and like many teens with similar diagnoses, she had grown accustomed to being misunderstood. Most of her life had been lived in that invisible space between presence and absence, where people were near, but never quite knew how to meet her where she actually lived.

But something shifted in those three days.

On day one, she sat hunched in her chair, knees together, arms crossed over her lap, trying to disappear into the folds of her hoodie. She barely spoke, and when she did, her words were tentative, floating just above a whisper. But by day two, I noticed her sitting taller. Not forced. Not trying to impress. Just... taller. Her spine had unwound itself without her even realizing it. There was a stillness in her now, not from fear, but from presence. She began walking with a smoother rhythm, a subtle new confidence in her steps. And the eye contact, something that had been impossible for more than a few seconds, now lingered. Minutes, even. She would meet my gaze, hold it, and stay there. It was like she had found something safe in the room and decided she no longer needed to hide.

But the shift wasn't only hers. Her mother had come with her to the class. And if the daughter had arrived with a quiet nervous system, the mother had arrived with a loud one. Worry hummed in her field like electricity. You could feel the exhaustion in her bones, the tightness in her jaw, the tension in her protectiveness. Like many parents of children on the spectrum, she carried a silent burden: the fear that she had somehow failed, that her daughter's differences were her fault, that love required constant vigilance and over-functioning. There was love, no doubt. But it had become entangled with guilt and control.

But something began to melt in her, too.

As she watched her daughter shift, posture changing, presence deepening, connection forming, something inside her started to soften. She began to trust her daughter in a new way, not out of resignation, but reverence. She started to see the blessing instead of the burden. She began to see her daughter not as a project to fix, but as a soul carrying wisdom that didn't fit the mold of the world but was no less divine.

The change in the daughter catalyzed a change in the mother. And that shift reverberated even further. Their family had been struggling in more ways than one. There had been tension in the marriage, quiet conflict beneath the surface. Blame. Distance. The kind of emotional disconnect that creeps in slowly when life feels heavy and you don't know how to name what hurts. But now, something was loosening in the roots.

What I've found, again and again, is that many couples with a neurodivergent child unconsciously turn their pain into conflict. They don't mean to. But when you view a condition like autism through the lens of burden, it creates pressure. It creates guilt. It creates cycles of martyrdom, resentment, and withdrawal. The child becomes a silent battlefield where the marriage slowly unravels. And yet, when one parent begins to see the condition as sacred, not in a romanticized way, but in a soul-level way, everything changes.

I'm a believer in the scripture that says everything under Heaven has a purpose. And while I've wrestled with that in my own life more than once, when I slow down and feel into it, I can see the truth there. Even pain has purpose. Even discomfort is a messenger. But for that to be more than just a spiritual idea, it has to live inside of me as truth. When I work with clients, I can't fake that belief; I have to embody it. Everything is a blessing. That has to be my baseline. If it's not, I can't hold the kind of space that creates a fundamental transformation.

So, with this mother, father, and daughter, I imagined something bigger than the story of diagnosis and dysfunction. I imagined three souls who chose one another before time began, who came into this lifetime to help each other remember. Not remember facts or data, but remember God. Remember wholeness. Remember what it means to love beyond roles, beyond appearances, beyond conditions.

And if that's true, if their daughter's autism is not a problem to solve but a portal to walk through, then every moment of pain was a sacred invitation to go deeper. Every moment of frustration, a doorway into greater compassion. Every emotional trigger, a reminder of how much healing is still possible.

I know it may sound strange to say, but I've found pain to be one of the clearest guides to love. The more intense the pain, the greater the potential for transformation. Pain clarifies. It reveals. And eventually, if we let it, it humbles us into gratitude.

As pain dissolves, awareness expands. And what was once unbearable becomes illuminating.

And when we begin to appreciate the small things, the eye contact, the posture shift, the softened voice, gratitude grows. And that gratitude begins to transform more than just the individual. It starts changing entire systems. Families. Relationships. Futures.

The mother who once blamed herself began to forgive herself. She began to see her daughter's strength. She stopped trying to do everything for her. She began stepping out of codependency and into trust. She stopped walking through her daughter's autism *for* her and started walking *with* her. And in doing so, she and her husband began healing their own emotional rigidity. In a way, they began walking through their own "autism," their patterns of disconnection, control, and fear, and stepping into deeper levels of curiosity, presence, and play.

This is what happens when the body feels secure.

When the soul feels seen.

When the story is rewritten.

Healing doesn't always look like a cure; sometimes it looks like a girl standing taller, a mother letting go, a family remembering how to love each other again.

And sometimes, that is the greatest miracle of all.

Cognitive Decline for 15 Years to Functioning Again

I've worked with many individuals over the years who were struggling with memory loss, mental fog, and cognitive breakdown, not just minor forgetfulness, but deeply rooted decline that left them unable to function in daily life. Some couldn't remember appointments, conversations, or even simple tasks. Others had trouble focusing, completing goals, or maintaining any real sense of momentum. But there was one man in particular who stood out. Not just because of the depth of his symptoms, but because of what emerged through our work together.

When I met him, he was sixty-four years old. He had not been able to work for over fifteen years. He couldn't manage even the simplest errands without help. Going to the grocery store had become a humiliating ordeal. He would walk in and forget why he was there. Forget what he needed. Forget how to navigate the aisles. His world had become small, disorienting, and filled with the frustration of a mind that seemed to be slipping further away by the day.

But what was even more striking than the forgetfulness was the emotional pattern running beneath it. Whenever I asked him a question, anything from what he desired in life to what he had eaten that day, his response was always the same: "I don't know, I can't remember." And then he would cry. Every time. Those phrases weren't just words. They were walls. Emotional escape hatches he had used for decades.

What I came to realize is that this pattern didn't start when the cognitive issues began. This wasn't just neurological. It was behavioral. Learned. Practiced. For years, maybe even most of his adult life, he had used "I don't know" and "I can't remember" as a way to avoid discomfort. When his wife asked him questions, he didn't want to answer, when his children challenged him, when life pressed in, those phrases became his shield. His retreat. And over time, the mind followed the language.

Because words are never neutral. They carry weight. Repetition becomes reality.

The more he said, "I don't know," the more his system began to align with that truth. Until eventually, he honestly didn't know. His brain stopped searching for answers. His memory stopped working. His confidence dissolved. His language had hypnotized his body into forgetting who he was.

When someone lives in victimhood long enough, it becomes more than a mindset. It becomes a chemistry. A posture. A lens through which they view the world. And when that victim pattern has been passed down through generations, when "I don't know" is inherited, modeled, and normalized, it can feel almost impossible to see through it. But what I've learned is that no soul chooses a lineage by accident. If we hold the belief that everything is a blessing, then even these patterns, especially the painful ones, have purpose.

This man didn't just show up in that family line randomly; his soul chose it. Chose the dysfunction, the forgetting, the avoidance. Not as punishment. But as invitation. To be the one who remembers. To be the one who reverses the current and reclaims clarity. To take the broken threads and weave them into something whole.

That's what healing lineage really is. One soul helping another remember. One voice reintroducing light into the silence. It's never about blame. It's always about remembrance.

And so, in our first session, I didn't ask him to tell me about his past. I didn't ask him to explain his condition or recall the origin of his symptoms. I simply asked him to say something different.

"I can."

That was it.

Not "I'm healed." Not "I remember everything." Just "I can."

But even that was hard. You could see it in his face. Saying "I can" was like trying to push a boulder up a hill. His throat tightened. His eyes welled up. He sat frozen for a long time, as if his body didn't know how to compute those two words. And then, with effort, he spoke them.

"I can."

Soft. Fragile. But real.

And again.

"I can."

This wasn't affirmation. This wasn't recitation. This was the beginning of something sacred. A new sound frequency entering a space that had been saturated with fear and defeat. The more he said it, the more his emotional field began to shift. His breathing deepened. His face softened. Something old and heavy began to lift. And for the first time in a long time, he wasn't crying from helplessness. He was crying from possibility.

Here's what most people miss: Healing isn't about pretending; it's about alignment. The words must be matched to the feeling, and then the feeling must match the intention. And when all three come into resonance, words, emotion, belief, that is when the body responds. That's when the subconscious listens. That's when transformation becomes instantaneous.

Because in that moment, you're not repeating something to try to change your life. You're speaking from the truth that already exists. And when your body hears that truth, it moves. It shifts. It re-patterns.

That's what began to happen in this man.

He started to see a flicker of a new life, one in which he was capable. Clear. Present. One in which he wasn't defined by the story of decline but energized by the story of becoming. And as he continued practicing this simple reversal, "I can," the fog began to lift. His cognitive function began to improve. His ability to engage with the world returned, not all at once, but steadily. His wife noticed it. His energy changed. His mood lifted. He smiled more.

This was not the result of years of therapy. This was not a pharmaceutical shift. This was a soul remembering what it had forgotten, and the body responding in kind.

The moment a person begins to re-engage with life, life responds.

The moment they stop resigning and start resonating, something in the field opens up. Synchronicities happen. Energy rises. Function returns. But it all begins with language. Not surface-level, not robotic, but language that is felt, that is meant, that is owned.

This is the power of speaking from the end. This is the essence of transformation.

And this man, once lost in the fog of "I can't remember," began to see the sun again.

Not just in his thoughts.

But in his body.

In his life.

In his future.

Chapter 11: Rewiring Your Relationship to Life: Healing Through Unity

Why QLT™ Works Across Health, Wealth, and Relationships

Why does QLT work across every area of life, health, wealth, relationships, and more? Because it doesn't just address symptoms. It rewires how a person relates to Life itself.

Not life with a lowercase "l," the to-do list, the bills, the job title, the circumstances. I'm talking about Life with a capital "L," the living intelligence behind everything. The breath of Being. The field of consciousness we're all immersed in, whether we're aware of it or not.

The power of QLT isn't in fixing what's wrong; it's in transforming the individual's relationship with that field.

Every person already has a relationship with Life. Whether they know it or not, they are in constant conversation with it, through their thoughts, their words, their emotions, and especially their beliefs. And most people are walking around in a dysfunctional relationship with Life, just like they might be in a dysfunctional relationship with a partner. They expect Life to let them down. To betray them. To abandon them. Or they think they have to earn Life's approval. Perform for its love. Suffer for its blessings.

But once that person begins to see the truth, really see it, their entire experience begins to shift. They realize that what they've been calling "life" was just their filtered interpretation of it. And as the lens changes, the field responds.

This is why QLT works whether someone is struggling with chronic illness, financial stress, or emotional trauma. Because underneath every issue is the same thing: a fractured relationship with Life.

When someone begins to heal that relationship, they begin to heal everything else, too.

And the way they do that is by starting to appreciate Life. Not just in theory, but viscerally. When appreciation takes root, it changes chemistry. It shifts the brain's wiring. It alters the frequency of the body. The person begins to notice beauty again. Little things, sunlight through a window, a smile from a stranger, the feeling of breath in the lungs. These aren't small. These are the early signs of awakening.

And as appreciation expands, so does awareness.

The inner dialogue starts to shift. The old story, "I'm not good enough," "I can't get it right," "It never works out for me," begins to dissolve. Not because someone forced it away, but because it can't survive in the atmosphere of truth. In its place, something new begins to rise.

"I am."

"I can."

"I love."

"I create."

"I enjoy."

These aren't affirmations. These are frequencies. They don't just decorate the mind, they reorganize reality.

As the person speaks them, feels them, and begins to embody them, they come into deeper and deeper recognition that they are not just a character in their life. They are the writer. The director. The producer. The camera crew. They begin to remember that they are the one shaping the scene. And the scene starts to shift.

That's the power of this work. It doesn't matter if the person is thirty or eighty. If they're willing, truly willing, to explore something new, or if they're in enough pain that they're ready to let go of what's familiar, they can experience this transformation.

I've worked with people in their mid to late seventies, even some in their early eighties, who began to discover this for the first time. Can you imagine? Living eight decades thinking life is something that happens to you, random, unfair, out of your control, and then one day waking up to realize it was never that way at all. That you've been co-creating it all along.

And now, finally, you see the thread.

The pattern.

The mirror.

The invitation.

That shift alone changes everything.

Because from that place, even if they only have a few years left on this earth, they live them in awe. In wonder. In appreciation. They don't leave this life bitter, resigned, or reluctant. They leave it whole. Grateful. Softened by the beauty, they finally allowed themselves to see.

And what a gift that is.

To leave the planet not feeling wasted or defeated, but with a heart full of reverence. To feel the breath of Life and say, "Thank you." To recognize that the story wasn't about surviving. It was about remembering. About reconnecting with what never left.

That's why QLT isn't just for the body. It's not just for money. It's not just for relationship healing.

It's for remembering how to live.

It's for remembering how to love.

And most of all, it's for remembering that you are the one who gets to choose how this life unfolds.

Coherence in the System: How Everything Is Connected

We're living in an extraordinary time, one when science is finally catching up to what mystics, healers, and sages have been saying for centuries: We are all connected. Every part of the system influences every other part. There is no such thing as isolation, not at the level of biology, not at the level of energy, and certainly not at the level of consciousness.

What we shift within ourselves doesn't stay confined to us. It echoes. It reverberates through the collective, through the unseen strands of the quantum field. This is not just poetic metaphor. This is physics. Biology. Chemistry. Frequency.

And the system we're working with here, the QLT, functions not because it is some magical outlier, but because it aligns with the most profound truth of the universe: Everything is connected.

There's a famous example of this that I often return to, not because it's a neat little metaphor, but because it happened. During the era of atomic testing in the Pacific, nuclear bombs were detonated on a group of islands. The land became irradiated, lifeless and contaminated. Scientists wanted to study how long it would take for life to return, so they reintroduced animal species, including monkeys. The fruit on the islands was coated in radioactive dust, and the monkeys, unaware, began eating it. Many became ill. Some died.

But then something fascinating occurred.

Researchers began teaching a small group of monkeys on one island to wash the fruit before eating it. And as more monkeys learned, something crossed a mysterious threshold. Around the time the hundredth monkey learned this new behavior, monkeys on all the surrounding islands, who had no physical contact with the first group, began washing their fruit, too.

No one had taught them. No one had modeled it. It simply emerged.

This became known as the "Hundredth Monkey Effect," the idea that when a critical mass of individuals internalizes a new behavior or insight, it suddenly becomes available to the collective. Not through books or broadcasts, but through the morphogenetic field, the invisible web that connects us all. One shift becomes our shift.

There's another story, this one closer to the mind.

A chemistry professor once gave his students a set of instructions for a lab experiment. The instructions contained an error: The combination of chemicals should not have produced any reaction. But because the professor told them it would, and because every student believed it would, nearly all of them reported the expected outcome. In other words, the belief produced the result. The body, the mind, the chemistry, all responded to the energetic imprint of expectation.

This same phenomenon shows up constantly in medicine. The placebo effect isn't a footnote to the drug trial. In many cases, it matches or even exceeds the effectiveness of the pharmaceutical. Why? Because when someone believes they are receiving medicine, their biology responds accordingly. The nervous system relaxes. The chemistry shifts. The healing begins, not because of what was swallowed, but because of what was believed.

You've probably experienced this in your own life; we all have. A moment when something changed that shouldn't have. When a result came out of nowhere. When healing happened faster than it "should have." And our tendency is to chalk it up to luck or call it a miracle. Something outside of us. Something unrepeatable.

But when we do that, we unintentionally cut ourselves off from doing it again.

The truth is, you did something. You shifted something. You aligned with something larger. And instead of brushing it off, what if you paused and asked, *what did I do, consciously or unconsciously, to create that outcome?*

When you ask that question with sincerity, Life answers. And in that answer is your power.

Because once you realize what you did once, you can begin to do it again.

And then again.

And then on purpose.

You build trust not through control, but through observation. Through pattern recognition. Through reverence. And the more your confidence grows, in yourself, in Life, in God, in Source, in this unseen brilliance that holds everything together, the more your manifestations begin to accelerate. Not just in frequency, but in scale. Your results become bolder. Faster. More aligned. Not because you're "trying harder," but because you're moving in coherence with the system itself.

And as your results grow, so does your respect for the process.

So does your gratitude.

So does your awe.

You begin to realize this isn't a personal journey. This is a collective evolution. Every time you heal something within yourself, you shift something in the collective. Every time you reclaim power from victimhood, that frequency becomes more available for others. Every time you remember who you are, you help the entire system remember, too.

This is why healing is never the final goal; it's the byproduct, the natural outcome of becoming coherent, internally and with Life itself. It's the fruit that ripens when your roots are deep in truth.

So don't dismiss the synchronicities. Don't brush off the breakthroughs. Don't call them luck or miracles.

Call them proof that everything is connected.

Call them invitations.

Call them yours.

Because they are.

And they always have been.

The Real Goal: Peace, Presence, and Purpose

When we use the word goal, we often don't realize how subtly it tricks us. It implies there's something out there, some future state, achievement, or arrival point, that will finally make us whole. It seduces us into chasing, performing, striving. It tells us, *You're not there yet. And if you're not careful, you'll live your whole life believing that the joy, peace, and fulfillment you crave live on the other side of some distant outcome.*

This is one of the deepest illusions keeping humanity stuck: the belief that peace is earned. That presence must be waited for. That purpose only begins once we "get there." But the truth is the opposite. Healing, wholeness, even joy all begin the moment we choose to live from purpose, not for it.

To live a fulfilled life requires purpose, but not in the way most people define it. A goal without a purpose is hollow. It may impress others, but it won't fulfill the soul. Purpose, true purpose, is not about what you achieve; it's about what you love. It's about the state of being you most desire to embody and share. It's the experience that lights you up from the inside out, and in doing so, radiates that same light to those around you.

Purpose is the feeling you love experiencing within yourself, expressed through the world.

For example, I love awakening enthusiasm in the people I meet. That moment when someone's eyes widen, their breath catches, and their energy shifts. It's subtle, but electric. When I feel that flicker of life ignite in someone else, it awakens more of it in me. It becomes a loop of aliveness: My enthusiasm feeds theirs; theirs feeds mine. And suddenly, we're both more awake than we were a moment ago.

That's what a purpose feels like. Not a job. Not a role. But a lived current. A state of resonance with what makes you feel most alive.

And when you're living from purpose, when you're not waiting to reach it, but allowing it to guide your actions, your words, your choices, something incredible happens: Peace arrives.

Not the peace of circumstances, but the peace of coherence.

In that peace, there's nothing to fix. No one to change. No race to run. Things still happen. Life still moves. But it unfolds from a different place. Your experience becomes a reflection of your inner decree.

Whatever arises come from within your own alignment.

This is the beginning of presence, the ability to remain in deep awareness of your internal chemistry. Not just your thoughts, but your feelings. The subtle sensations. The tension or ease in your shoulders. The flutter in your gut. The expansion in your chest. Presence is the art of listening inward with curiosity and love. It's noticing what your energy is doing, how your body is responding, how your frequency is influencing those around you, and doing it when it matters most.

Presence isn't just a meditative state. It's leadership. It's relational. It's alchemical. It is your ability to observe and choose your way into aligned action.

And when someone is living from presence and purpose, they no longer need to "find" their power; they *are* it. They become more sensitive to what takes them out of that alignment. They begin to recognize the tasks, thoughts, and distractions that create noise, static in the system. And they start to let those things go. Not with resistance, but with clarity.

The delay dissolves. The excuses soften. They begin walking with single vision, moving their unique blessing through them, into the world.

This is why purpose must be deeply felt, not adopted as an idea, but embraced as an experience.

It's not about doing what looks meaningful. It's about doing what feels like life pulsing through you.

Some people say that anything that takes you away from your life purpose is noise; others say it's part of the journey. I believe both can be true. But eventually, the more you live in alignment with what you love, the more noise falls away on its own. You stop needing to convince yourself to focus, because focus is the natural byproduct of living what matters.

And so, the real goal is never the outcome. It's the state.

Peace is not a place you arrive at.

Presence is not a performance.

Purpose is not a job title.

They are qualities of being.

And when they are lived, not talked about, but felt, chosen, embodied, they become the doorway through which everything else flows. Health, wealth, love, and creativity all rise through coherence.

So instead of asking, "What should I do with my life?"

Try asking, "What do I love feeling that also lights up the people around me?"

And start there.

Let that be your compass. Let that be your goal.

And let the rest unfold as the gift it was always meant to be.

Chapter 12: Your DNA Is Listening

Frequency and the Body: Rewriting Chemistry

The human body is a breathtaking system, resilient, adaptive, intelligent. It's not just flesh and bone. It's a living container for consciousness, a biological masterpiece that, as scripture reminds us, serves as the temple of the Living God. And like any true temple, it's designed not just to shelter life, but to respond to it.

Our bodies can survive in the most extreme conditions. People have built lives in the frozen stillness of the Arctic and in the blistering heat of the desert. Communities have thrived in lush river valleys and dry, cracked plains where water is scarce and the sun is unforgiving. No matter where we go, we adapt. We evolve. We survive. That's the miracle of the design. But while our bodies can adapt to physical climates, what many people overlook is how deeply our biology responds to our mental climate: our beliefs, our language, our emotions, and the frequency we hold.

Across every culture, in every language, there are common archetypal conversations that quietly shape the nervous system. "I'm not good enough." "Life is hard." "Nothing ever works out for me." These aren't just thoughts; they're codes. And the more we rehearse them, the more they imprint themselves into the brain, firing the same neural pathways again and again until those circuits become the default setting.

When someone's internal dialogue is rooted in victimhood, their body doesn't stay unaffected; it adapts to match that belief. The brain begins to shut out possibilities. The chemistry shifts toward survival. The cells become more rigid, inflamed, closed. The deeper the victim mentality, the greater the cellular toxicity. What begins as a belief becomes a biological state.

But here's the good news: The body also responds to truth.

To rewrite chemistry, a person doesn't need to become perfect; they just need to become willing: willing to try a new perspective, willing to soften their grip on the familiar, even when the familiar has been laced with pain. Most people don't realize how deeply they've been programmed, not just by trauma or personal experience, but by generations of societal scripts, scripts handed down through family dynamics, religious dogma, school systems, and cultural traditions that taught people what to think instead of how to think.

Many of us were rewarded for repeating what we were told, not for questioning it. We were taught to memorize, regurgitate, and conform. And when someone in the system finally says, "This doesn't feel true," they're often met with resistance. They're told they're being difficult. Unfaithful. Disrespectful. But in truth, they're waking up.

It takes courage to question the collective. Especially when those questions challenge the status quo. Throughout history, those who have dared to think for themselves have been mocked, exiled, even executed. To go against the crowd is to face the full force of society's cognitive dissonance. And yet, awakening always begins this way: with one voice willing to say, "What if that's not true?"

And not just externally. That dissonance arises inside the individual, too. When someone begins to wake up to the lies they've been living in, whether they came from a preacher, a teacher, a parent, or their own ego, a kind of internal chaos can set in. The old belief system begins to fracture, and the body feels it. The nervous system may react. Doubt creeps in. But underneath that noise, something deeper is stirring: the frequency of truth.

One of the fastest ways to bring that truth online is through decrees: spoken affirmations, but more powerful. Not words you hope are true, but words you are willing to try on as a new internal standard. Decrees like:

I love truth. Truth speaks through me. I give myself permission to see truth.

These aren't fluffy mantras; they are frequency-setting tools. And when spoken from the heart, when repeated with intention, they begin to shift everything, from the language of the cells to the emotions that rise. But here's the part no one tells you: The moment you begin declaring truth, you will likely feel the pain of every lie that truth is replacing.

That's part of the process. The pain isn't punishment; it's purification. The body is detoxing old distortions.

The person begins to realize: "I didn't just believe these lies; I built a life around them. I made decisions from them. I raised children in them. I betrayed myself to maintain them." That's not easy to face. But it's freeing. And on the other side of that honesty is peace.

Because once you feel the peace of truth, even if just for a moment, it becomes your new reference point. Your body remembers it. Your nervous system begins recalibrating to it. The chemicals shift. The cells open. The entire system begins to rewrite itself, not from effort, but from coherence.

And that's the key.

You don't need to fix the body. You need to speak to it differently.

You don't need to fight your programming; you need to recode it.

Your biology is listening. Your DNA is listening. And when it hears truth, it responds.

So, the next time you feel like giving in to the old narrative, try this instead:

Pause. Breathe. Speak a new decree.

Then listen to your body.

Watch your emotions.

Notice your thoughts.

And let the frequency of truth do what it was always meant to do: restore you.

The Brain, The Body, and the Invisible Realm

The healthier our brain and body are, the healthier our conversations become. Not just the ones we have with others, but the ones we have with ourselves, the ones we don't even realize we're listening to all day long.

See, the brain isn't just an organ of thought. It's a bioelectrical, biofeedback-responsive masterpiece. It is constantly scanning the internal and external environment, assessing safety, storing memory, regulating emotion, and assigning meaning. And if the chemistry inside the body is distorted, if the field is flooded with stress hormones and cellular toxicity, the messages we receive from the brain get scrambled. Our perception shifts. Truth becomes harder to access. Our reality becomes narrowed by the frequency we're tuned into.

When we are depleted, physically, emotionally, or spiritually, the brain doesn't shut off. It just loops. It starts playing old recordings. Repetitive thoughts. Familiar complaints. The "I can't," "It's too hard," "Nothing ever changes" kind of loops that aren't just annoying, they're chemically addictive. The more stress you're under, the more your body loses essential minerals, and the more those minerals drain, the harder it becomes to generate new thoughts. It's like trying to change the station with a broken dial.

That's why so much of the QLT™ includes mineralizing the body. It's not just about nutrition. It's about reclaiming the biological foundation for change. When the body is properly supported, and the brain is fed, everything gets clearer. The fog begins to lift. The static dissolves. The loops begin to quiet. And instead of defaulting to complaint, the individual begins accessing solutions. Action becomes natural. Discernment returns.

One of the core principles of QLT is this: effective action.

That doesn't mean busyness. It means alignment. It means the person isn't just reacting from the old programming, parroting whatever fear the news is selling that week, or recycling the drama of childhood wounds. Instead, they become sovereign. Present. Awake. They begin to see that they are the cause, not the victim, of the energy they bring into the world.

And as that sovereignty grows, so does their capacity. Not just to function, but to thrive. Their body improves. Their relationships stabilize. Their home environment softens. And because we're all connected, their personal coherence begins to ripple outward. The family shifts. The community responds. Society, slowly but surely, begins to change.

But it always begins with the individual.

True collective healing cannot be top-down; it must rise from within. And that rise requires that each person cleanse their own inner toxicity, that they stop waiting for someone else to fix it, that they stop blaming. Because the chemistry you carry is the lens through which you view the world. If you're walking around with suppressed anger, resentment, or judgment, then your nervous system will filter reality to match it. You'll only see what confirms your pain.

It's like changing the channel, but the remote is your emotional body.

When you're angry, you see betrayal. When you're afraid, you see danger. When you're unworthy, you see rejection. And someone else, standing in the exact same circumstance, might see beauty, possibility, or a lesson. The difference is not the event; it's the meaning we assign to it, the chemistry we're soaking in, the story we're still believing.

I often tell a story in my classes to demonstrate this. Imagine lining up twenty people on a stage. You walk down the line and slap each one of them across the cheek with the exact same force, in the exact same spot. How many reactions do you think you'd get?

At least 20 answers.

Maybe more, depending on how many emotions are living under the surface. One person might laugh. Another might freeze. One might cry. Another might retaliate. Some may cycle through two or three reactions. But here's the point: The event was the same for everyone. The difference is how each person interpreted the event. And that interpretation comes from the emotional wiring of the individual, not from the truth of the moment.

So, when someone has an outburst during a disagreement with their spouse and says, "You're just like my dad," the reality is not that their partner is their dad; it's that the unresolved pain of their past has hijacked their present. The person they married might actually be perfect for them, not because they avoid triggering them, but because they bring those triggers to the surface. So, they can finally be healed.

But instead of seeing that opportunity, most people project. They blame. They leave.

What if there were a way to use that trigger, not to spiral, but to evolve?

That's what QLT offers: a path to alchemize reactivity into conscious choice. Instead of repeating old reactions that were hardwired in childhood, you begin choosing responses rooted in love, clarity, and present-day awareness. You begin living not from the wounds of your past, but from the wisdom of your soul.

Now imagine what this could do for our culture. Imagine a generation of children raised by adults who were not at war with themselves. Adults who no longer projected their shame, their fear, their guilt onto their kids. Adults who could hold space for anger without collapsing into it. Who could model responsibility, discernment, emotional fluency. Imagine children who are conceived with intention, carried with reverence, and raised not to be controlled, but to be cherished.

If that were our new normal, there would be no pro-life versus pro-choice debate. Because the child would never be a battleground for someone else's pain. The child would be sacred. And the adult would be ready.

All of this begins with emotional responsibility, with the willingness to see beyond good and bad, right and wrong. Those are the programs that keep the brain stuck in fight or flight. They keep the nervous system hijacked. They keep the species divided.

But when we take our attention off the binary, off the battle, and place it on the actual result we choose to experience, something new becomes available: A different timeline opens, one where peace is possible. One where the nervous system no longer needs to defend itself against truth. One where the invisible realm of frequency becomes the bridge between the world we inherited and the one we're here to create.

And it starts in the brain.

It lives in the body.

But it is always activated in the invisible.

Manifestation as a Biological Process

Manifestation is not just a metaphysical idea. It is not something reserved for vision boards, lucky breaks, or the spiritual elite. Manifestation is happening in real time, every moment, inside your body. It is a biological process, grounded in chemistry, shaped by frequency, and reflected through your physical experience.

We were born with the gift of creation. Every single one of us. From the moment our cells began dividing in the womb, we were manifesting, generating new matter, organizing life, participating in a complex dance of intelligence we didn't have to earn. Co-creation isn't a special skill for the spiritually inclined; it's embedded in our DNA.

Even now, as you read these words, your body is manifesting. It's creating. Thousands of new cells are forming in your blood, your skin, your bones. And those cells don't form in a vacuum. They form in the biochemical soup that you carry within you. That soup is flavored by your emotions, your thoughts, your food, your memories, your beliefs. The body doesn't just respond to what you eat; it responds to what you feel. It listens to the words you speak. It reacts to what you fear and what you love. That's what I mean when I say your DNA is listening. It is listening to you.

And what it hears, it translates into matter.

If you are living in a constant state of stress, anger, or low-grade resentment, your cells adapt to that environment. Your body begins to normalize it. You get used to the static. You stop noticing the drama. The same way a person addicted to heroin slowly needs more and more of the drug to feel the same high, the body addicted to stress needs more chaos to feel "alive."

That's how trauma becomes identity. That's how dysfunction becomes familiar. That's how people get addicted to drama, not because they love suffering, but because their biology has acclimated to it. They don't know any other way to feel real.

And the body? It keeps manifesting according to the conditions it's given.

This is why so many people manifest pain even when they're asking for healing. They manifest lack even while visualizing abundance. They manifest conflict while declaring they want peace. It's not because they're broken. It's because their chemistry is communicating one thing while their words are requesting another. The universe doesn't respond to what we want. It responds to who we are being, right now, in the body, in the nervous system, in the field.

This is why ease matters. Not just as a concept, but as a biological condition.

The more ease you embody, the more ease becomes your baseline. You begin to see it reflected in your relationships, in your finances, in your health. When you're anchored in the parasympathetic state, the body's state of rest, restoration, and creative power, you become magnetic to solutions. You respond to challenges from clarity, not panic. You become someone who can walk into a chaotic room and bring coherence, not because you're better, but because you're regulated.

But most people aren't living from that state. They're stuck in fight or flight. They've conditioned themselves to operate in survival mode. And so they unknowingly chase the emotional equivalent of their drug, an argument, a crisis, a problem to fix, because that's the chemistry their system recognizes as "home." That's what feels familiar. That's what feels safe.

In sympathetic dominance, the body isn't interested in vision; it's interested in protection. You'll find yourself complaining, blaming, reacting, defending. You'll create more of what you fear, then use the chaos as evidence that the world is unsafe. That's how the loop sustains itself. That's how the body becomes the manifestation engine of your pain.

And because the nervous system is so fast, it begins to confuse this loop for identity. The person doesn't just say "I feel angry." They say, "I am an angry person." They don't just say "I've experienced struggle." They say, "Life is hard." The emotion fuses with the ego and becomes who they believe they are.

But this can change. And it changes faster than we were taught.

When the body shifts into parasympathetic, into a state of safety and presence, consciousness expands. New ideas come. The individual stops fighting the past and starts asking, "What would I love to create?" From that state, manifestation becomes natural. Joyful. Precise. Because it's no longer distorted by fear. It's no longer filtered through survival mode. It's no longer being jammed through the chemistry of trauma.

You've probably seen this before, maybe in someone who just feels light. They move through life with grace. They don't rush. They don't explode. They don't over-explain. They bring a calm that you can feel in your bones. These people aren't lucky; they're regulated. And that regulation allows them to manifest without force.

They walk into a room and the solution shows up. They think of someone and that person calls. Their body heals without a fight. That's not magic. That's coherence.

And the good news is, it's available to you.

Manifestation is not something you "do." It's something you allow, something you become. It's the natural byproduct of an internally aligned system. When your thoughts, feelings, chemistry, and identity are in harmony, when your nervous system feels secure enough to create, manifestation becomes inevitable.

But to get there, we must willing to break the addiction to stress, to stop identifying with our complaints, to stop rehearsing our pain like it's a badge of honor, to stop manifesting from the sympathetic nervous system. Because as long as we're surviving, we cannot fully create.

So, the real work isn't to hustle harder or visualize longer.

The real work is to feel securer in your own body.

That's where everything begins. That's where biology meets destiny. That's where manifestation moves from theory into experience. That's where you stop trying to control the future and start collaborating with the present.

And from that place, ease becomes natural. Abundance becomes obvious. Health becomes normal. Love becomes home.

Because the body finally remembers what it was designed to do.

Create.

Chapter 13: The QLT™ Client Map

How to Identify Which Area Requires a Leap

Not everything requires a leap. But anything you're tolerating would benefit from one.

Anywhere you're asking how, how you're going to do something, how you're going to make something work, how you'll survive it, fix it, push through, it's often a subtle signal. The frequency of how is rarely rooted in presence. It's rooted in pressure. In grasping. In the silent belief that life isn't already working for you, so you'll have to figure it out on your own.

That's a perfect place for a leap.

Any time you find yourself carrying a low-grade hum of dissatisfaction, putting up with something that drains you, steals your time, dulls your radiance, that's a signal too. Tolerations are slow leaks. They erode energy and erode vision. They whisper, "This is fine," when your soul is saying, "This is not it."

And when you catch yourself complaining, not once, but over and over about the same thing? That's a flashing neon light.

A repeated complaint is not just a preference. It's not just venting. It's your body and field signaling that you're running energy through a pattern that no longer fits who you're becoming. And when your current behavior or story doesn't match your deeper knowing, friction occurs. That friction? It's the call. It's the invitation.

That's where a QLT becomes possible.

If you're in a relationship that feels heavy instead of light… if the laughter is fading… if the spark of playfulness or the ease of connection has slowly drained away… that's a place to look. Love is meant to expand us, not slowly harden us into obligation. If your relationship feels like a compromise of self, instead of a celebration of it, that's a place to leap.

If you're spending more time thinking about your bills than your income…

If your first instinct is to check your bank account before you check in with your desire…

If you've ever caught yourself calculating how many years you have left to live based on how much money is in your savings…

Those are all places.

They're not just symptoms. They're mirrors. Each one is showing you what you're living from, what you're agreeing to, what you're believing without question.

If you're facing health issues, or feel like your body is failing you, or you're numbing your system with pharmaceuticals or substances, there's a leap waiting. One that isn't just about the body, but about the field. About what energy you've been looping. What fear you've been carrying. What power you've forgotten belongs to you.

If you notice yourself snapping, at your partner, your kids, your parents, strangers, this too is a map. Those reactive patterns didn't come from nowhere. They are fragments of your past rising up for resolution. Not to shame you. But to wake you. To bring your awareness back to what's still operating behind the scenes.

Every unconscious reaction is a pointer toward a conscious leap.

And if you've buried a dream? If there's something you once imagined for yourself that you now talk about like it's ridiculous, irresponsible, or "for other people," that's a place to return to. Because nothing is more sacred than the dream that keeps whispering to you even after you've shut the door, that dream is not random. It's a map. It's coded into you for a reason.

So, ask yourself, right now:

Where am I tolerating what I no longer desire?

Where am I pretending this is just "how life is"?

Where do I complain, shrink, snap, or settle?

Where have I stopped dreaming because I forgot how to believe?

That's where your next leap lives.

It doesn't require struggle. It doesn't require figuring it all out. It only requires the willingness to see it, to feel where you've been living small, and to allow a new outcome to emerge from a different state of being.

In QLT, we don't chase problems. We don't analyze the past.

We look for these markers, these doorways.

And once we see the pattern clearly, we leap.

Not by force.

But by shifting the frequency.

By choosing a new result.

And letting the field reorganize around who we now are.

Because the leap never begins outside of you.

It begins in the moment you choose to stop tolerating what was never meant to be permanent.

It begins the moment you remember you were never meant to manage your pain.

You were born to transmute it into power.

The Daily Practice: Feeling, Speaking, Result

Here's a simple daily practice to begin shifting your field, right now.

It doesn't require hours of meditation. You don't need to wait for your next breakthrough session or escape into the mountains to feel clarity again. All you need is a pen, a sheet of paper, and a willingness to tell yourself the truth.

Begin like this: Fold the paper in half vertically, creating two columns. At the top of the left side, write:

"What I don't want / don't like."

This is the place for your "not" statements.

If you're under stress, if something in your life feels heavy or stuck or cyclical, start here. Get honest. Write them all down.

"I don't want to fight with my partner."

"I'm not making enough money."

"I don't want to feel tired all the time."

"I'm not happy in this job."

"I don't know how I'll ever get out of this."

Let it pour out. No censoring. No spiritual bypassing. No pretending it's not a thing when it clearly is.

You can even enlist your friends to help catch the "not" language in your everyday conversations. Be warned, though, if they're honest, you might get annoyed. Most of us have yet to realize how often we speak from what we don't want until someone reflects it back. It's like listening to a teenager who uses the word "like" every third word. At some point, you can't un-hear it.

And the same is true here.

Most people are unknowingly using the word "not" twenty, thirty, or even fifty times a minute.

And with every "not," the nervous system hears threat.

Every complaint, every focus on lack, sends a message to the subconscious: "We're not safe."

And when the subconscious hears that long enough, it starts re-creating more and more of what matches that belief.

That's how worry becomes a loop.

That's how stress manifests as more things to be stressed about.

It's the rat on the wheel, spinning faster and faster, convinced it's going somewhere, when it's just digging the groove deeper.

Now, look at your list of "not" statements.

On the right side of the page, write this heading:

"What I love / what I'm choosing."

Now, take each "not" statement from the left and rewrite it on the right side, this time, as a declaration of love, a conscious result, or a present-tense choice.

If you wrote:

"I don't want to fight with my partner,"

you might rewrite it as:

"I love speaking with my partner in a way that brings connection and peace,"

or, "I really love noticing the good in my partner and telling them."

If you wrote:

"I don't like having bills,"

try:

"I love having more than enough money to pay my bills with ease,"

or, "I love feeling supported and empowered in my finances."

When you first write these statements, they may feel false, fake, even laughable. That's okay; they're supposed to feel unnatural at first. They aren't describing your current circumstances. They're introducing a new frequency.

Think of it like planting seeds in a new garden. Of course, the flowers aren't visible yet. But that doesn't mean they're not already growing underground.

When you speak these "I love" statements out loud, and then follow them with a small, matching action, you begin to rewire the field.

For example:

Let's say you're paying a bill online. Instead of grumbling about it, pause. Place your hand on your heart. And say,

"Wow. I really love having the money to pay for this."

Or even just,

"I'm grateful I have this money right now."

It may seem small. But the subconscious is always listening.

And when you begin to attach gratitude, pleasure, and ease to things that previously felt like a burden or fear, you send a new command to the system:

We are secure.

We are provided for.

We live in ease.

And the subconscious doesn't argue. It just starts to believe you.

It updates the program.

You can do this with anything:

"I love my vibrant, healthy body."

"I love feeling supported by life."

"I love how easy it is to connect with people who get me."

"I love having the clarity and confidence to lead."

"I love the peace in our home."

Even if you're in the middle of a breakdown, you can speak from the breakthrough.

You don't have to know how.

You don't have to understand the steps.

You don't have to fix the problem or wait for someone else to change.

You just speak what you choose.

And then give yourself the feeling of it.

Feel the warmth in your chest.

The smile tugging at your lips.

The breath that drops down into your belly.

That's the secret.

You're not just reprogramming language.

You're imprinting the result through feeling.

You're teaching your nervous system what "truth" feels like.

Because the subconscious doesn't speak English.

It speaks emotions.

And the moment your words and your emotions line up, that's when everything starts to shift.

So today, grab a piece of paper.

One side: the "not"s.

The other: the "I love"s.

Say them out loud.

Feel them in your body.

Not as a performance. Not as a wish. But as a choice.

And then watch what happens when your inner reality stops fighting what is and starts becoming what you came here to create.

Remembering Unity in All Areas of Your Life

To bring unity into every area of your life, money, love, health, self, you get to first realize something radical:

You are not, and have never been, separate from it.

It is actually impossible to be out of unity. You can only create the experience of being out of unity. And you do that, ironically, by using your own power of unity to do so.

Let me explain.

What we label as separation, chaos, or lack is not a flaw in the design of life. It is a byproduct of what you have been unconsciously creating through your own alignment, your own agreement with separation. In other words, you used your gift of co-creation to produce an experience of disconnection, then believed the disconnection was real.

But it isn't. It never was. It's just a frequency you were tuned to.

Separation is a lens, not a law.

You can start to recognize this illusion through the words you speak. Pay attention to the language patterns that accompany the belief in lack. Certain phrases point directly to the internal story of disunity:

"I want…"

"I need…"

"I'm trying…"

"I'm hoping for…"

"I have to…"

"I should have…"

"I would have…"

"I could have…"

"I can't…"

Every time you say or think these phrases, you're broadcasting a message: "I am not whole. I am not in harmony. I am separate from what I desire."

And life, being the perfect mirror that it is, simply reflects your declaration. Not to punish you, but to lovingly show you the creative power you're wielding, even when you're unaware of it.

When you speak and feel from lack, life organizes itself to support that story. It isn't personal. It's just responsive. Life doesn't know how to contradict you. It only knows how to agree.

So, if you "want" to bring unity to money, to health, to your relationships, or your purpose, the first step is to become aware of how you've been using your words, and your feelings, to declare separation.

This is the invitation into mastery.

The invitation to realize, which literally means to "see with real eyes," that what you've been calling reality is not truth, but interpretation. It is perception filtered through programming. And once you realize that, you step into the role of the objective observer.

From this new vantage point, you are no longer the victim of circumstance; you're the one watching it unfold. You begin to notice the link between the words you use, the emotions you habitually carry, and the results you keep experiencing.

You begin to see how you've unconsciously created what you call
your life.

And here's the beautiful part: Once you see, you can choose again.

Even your so-called karmic manifestations, those deeply patterned,
automatic loops, begin to soften in the light of awareness. You see
your part in it, not with blame, but with clarity. You feel the sacred
weight of your own creative power.

And that's when gratitude becomes essential.

Gratitude is the bridge. The portal. The recalibration tool.

It doesn't just make you feel better. It tunes your frequency. It opens
your eyes to what's true beyond the illusion. Gratitude says, "Thank
you for letting me see what's real." It welcomes the correction, the
healing, the homecoming.

When it comes to bringing unity into specific areas like money or
health, it requires an understanding: Abundance is not something to
chase. It's something to remember.

You are already connected to the frequency of abundance. You just
forgot. And now, the practice is to re-attune your system to that
truth.

You do this by giving yourself the feeling of already having.

Not as a trick. Not as a performance. But as an embodied
declaration of what is already true in the unseen.

There is a scripture that says, "To the one who has, more will be
given. To the one who does not have, even what they have will be
taken."

It sounds harsh, until you understand it as a reflection of frequency.

When you feel like you have, you emit a signal of wholeness. Life responds to that. When you feel like you lack, even the things you do have begin to decay in your perception.

Ease in the body equals ease in life.

The more you cultivate internal coherence, gratitude, appreciation, presence, the more your outer world begins to match it. Money flows, health returns. Love becomes natural again. Not because you fought for it. But because you aligned with it.

I remember the exact moment this became viscerally true for me.

I was sitting in my office after a powerful coaching call. I had just gotten off Zoom, and I could feel something different in my body. It wasn't just excitement. It wasn't even joy. It was deeper. Softer. Quieter. But profoundly expansive.

I sat there, closed my eyes, and asked inside, "What is this feeling?"

And the word I heard was *reverence*.

That word was unfamiliar in my body. I had never consciously used it to describe how I felt about life. But in that moment, it landed like a sacred truth. The moment I spoke the word out loud, I started crying, not from sadness, but from the overwhelming sensation of being right with everything.

Reverence.

It shifted everything.

My nervous system dropped. My breath deepened. And for the first time in my adult life, I felt what it meant to honor life, not just talk about it. Not just perform gratitude. But to actually feel the holiness of being here. Alive. Awake. In relationship with this sacred unfolding.

I invite you to sit with that word for a moment. Say it out loud. Whisper it. Feel how it moves through your chest, your throat, your spine.

Reverence.

Let it teach you.

Let it soften you.

Let it remind you of who you were before you forgot. Before you split yourself into compartments. Before you tried to earn what was already yours.

Unity is not something to achieve.

It is the truth you return to when you drop the story of separation.

And from that place, every area of your life, money, love, health, purpose, begins to return home to you.

Not because you forced it.

Because you remembered what was always there to begin with.

The Quantum Leap of Remembrance

As you close the final pages of this book, I invite you to pause and realize there is a simplicity to Life of which most people have yet to discover. No matter how hard you try, it is impossible not to be manifesting. When this is realized, you may get a little scared about Life; however, you can shift the letters from *scared* to *sacred*. This is a powerful reframe and awakens gratitude and reverence for Life and your relationship with it. Cherish and keep this Truth in your Consciousness, especially if things appear to go awry. In these moments, apply the tools from QLT to quickly get back into your game of Life. Remember that it is okay to get triggered; the challenge is to see how quickly you can recover. QLT is designed for rapid deployment right in the middle of your kerfuffle. Remember that the more you can bring humor and enthusiasm to the situation, the faster and greater the transformation will be for you.

Through this journey, you have discovered a new way of being: one that transcends the paralyzing paradigm of right and wrong and empowers you to live from awareness, creation, and choice. This is your divine birthright, alive and resonant within every breath you take, ready to reshape your reality through conscious communion with the Source.

The stories, tools, and revelations you have encountered are not meant to linger on the page; they are a living invitation. These practices require commitment, embodiment, and mentorship to become your natural state of awareness. You now stand on the threshold of something far greater than understanding; you stand before remembrance itself. Through practice and faith, QLT will become your bridge to a frequency where limits dissolve, and creation becomes your language.

This is not an ending; it is a beginning. The quantum field is not somewhere out there. The field is us, and we are the field. Whatever we attempt to suppress and hide is revealed to us by our reflection in the 3D field.

Remember that everything we require is simply a frequency. Become the master of your own frequency to grow your conscious manifestations in boldness, greatness, and velocity.

Mark Scherer, PhD

Call to Action

Your Next Leap

The invitation is simple: Begin now.

To take the next step in integrating the Quantum Leap Technique™ and living from divine awareness, visit encompasslife.com and complete the connection form. A trained mentor will reach out to guide you in applying these tools with clarity, structure, and personalized support.

Transformation happens through practice. As you continue this work, you'll see evidence of change in every area of life: health, relationships, creativity, and purpose. Each shift reflects the deeper truth that you are never separate from the Source of all creation.

You are not broken, and you are not behind. You are awakening to what has always been within you: the power to choose, to create, and to live in alignment with divine order.

The movement has begun, and you are part of it.

Each person who awakens through remembrance contributes to the restoration of a world built on awareness, unity with God, and truth.

Are you ready for your next quantum leap?

Take the step. Trust the process. Remember who you are.

About the Author

Mark Scherer, PhD, is the founder of Encompass Life and the creator of the innovative Quantum Leap Technique™ (QLT). He holds a PhD in Transformational Life Coaching and Leadership Development from Aidan University and has spent more than 20 years guiding executives, entrepreneurs, healthcare professionals, and coaches toward rapid and meaningful personal and professional transformation.

Through QLT, Mark helps clients identify and release suppressed emotional patterns at the subconscious level—empowering them to break through long-standing barriers, reconnect with their core purpose, and move forward with renewed clarity and momentum. His philosophy of complete personal accountability and the principle of unity over duality cultivates heightened intuition, emotional intelligence, and an expanded sense of personal potential in those he serves.

With his authentic Texas roots, straightforward approach, and deep commitment to lasting transformation, Mark continues to impact lives and organizations around the world.

9 781969 888212